Learn to Code: Complete Commodore 64 Beginner's Guide

Enzo .R Villanueva

Funny helpful tips:

Stay proactive in understanding mixed reality; blending AR and VR, it offers immersive experiences with real-world interactions.

Stay adventurous; trying new things together keeps the spark alive.

Learn to Code: Complete Commodore 64 Beginner's Guide :
Master the Basics of Coding with this Comprehensive Guide to
Programming on the Iconic Commodore 64

Life advices:

Maintain a feedback loop with stakeholders; their insights are valuable.

Stay proactive in seeking out independent publishers; they often offer unique voices and perspectives.

Introduction

This is a comprehensive guide tailored for individuals new to coding on THEC64 computer. It is designed to provide a systematic introduction to the fundamentals of coding, gradually progressing from basic keyboard functions and navigation to more advanced programming concepts, including graphics, animation, sound effects, and music composition.

The guide begins with a thorough explanation of the keyboard layout, highlighting essential keys and their functionalities, such as RETURN, SHIFT, SHIFT LOCK, and various other keys crucial for programming on THEC64. It also covers important commands like CLR/HOME and RESTORE, enabling users to become familiar with the foundational aspects of THEC64's interface.

As users progress, they are introduced to the concept of programming on THEC64, learning to create their first program, and gaining insights into listing, editing, saving, and loading programs from virtual disks. Building on these foundational concepts, the guide then delves into various coding elements, including displaying numbers and text, incorporating colors, implementing calculations, and handling input and output operations.

The guide also provides comprehensive coverage of advanced programming techniques, such as loops, decision-making structures, memory management with POKE and PEEK commands, and the creation of character graphics and animation. It walks users through the intricacies of designing sprites, manipulating sprite colors and positions, and implementing sprite animation to enhance the visual appeal of their programs.

Furthermore, the guide offers a detailed exploration of sound programming on THEC64, focusing on creating sound effects, music, and chords, with in-depth discussions on the ADSR envelope, sound waveforms, notes, and frequency. It also covers the integration of special effects to further enrich the overall user experience.

Towards the end, the guide provides an overview of various display options, demonstrating how to draw backgrounds, play music, create animated sprites, and implement flashing borders, culminating in the creation of a fully functional main program. Additionally, it includes a comprehensive appendix covering the ASCII character set and error messages commonly encountered during the coding process.

Overall, this book serves as an invaluable resource for individuals looking to develop a strong foundational understanding of coding on THEC64, offering a structured and comprehensive approach to mastering the intricacies of programming on this platform.

Contents

THE KEYBOARD

RUN/STOP Stops a program that has been running and shows where it stopped. Use it with the SHIFT key to load a program from a cassette file.

CTRL Use it with the NUMBER keys 1-8 to access the eight colours marked on the keys. Used with keys 9 and 0 to produce reversed characters.

CLR/HOME Will move the cursor to the top left corner of the screen. Used with the SHIFT key, it will clear the screen.

RESTORE When used with the RUN/STOP key it will reset the computer back to the READY prompt.

INST/DEL Used for editing your program. On its own, it backspaces and deletes a character. Used with the SHIFT key, it inserts a space.

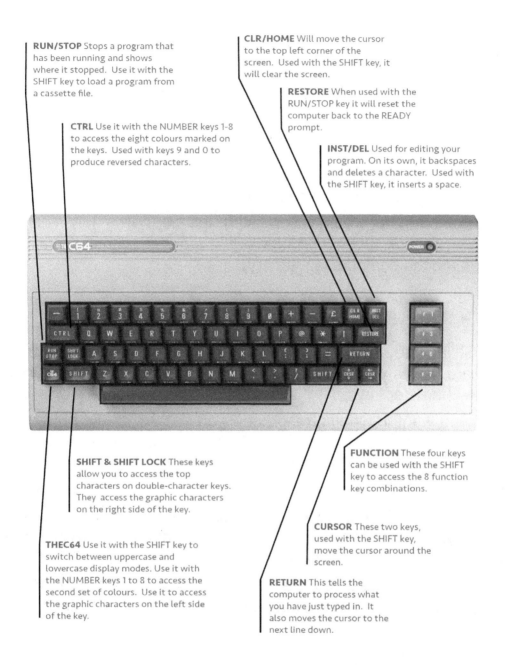

SHIFT & SHIFT LOCK These keys allow you to access the top characters on double-character keys. They access the graphic characters on the right side of the key.

THEC64 Use it with the SHIFT key to switch between uppercase and lowercase display modes. Use it with the NUMBER keys 1 to 8 to access the second set of colours. Use it to access the graphic characters on the left side of the key.

FUNCTION These four keys can be used with the SHIFT key to access the 8 function key combinations.

CURSOR These two keys, used with the SHIFT key, move the cursor around the screen.

RETURN This tells the computer to process what you have just typed in. It also moves the cursor to the next line down.

THEC64 keyboard is similar to any modern computer keyboard, but it has some keys and functions specific to running in BASIC mode. Let's take a closer look at these keys and functions.

RETURN

The RETURN key acts a little like the return or enter key on your regular computer keyboard by moving the cursor to a new line.

When entering a program, pressing the RETURN key tells the computer to look at what you have just typed in, check it and then enter it into the computer's memory.

SHIFT AND SHIFT LOCK

The SHIFT key works similar to that of a regular computer keyboard. It lets you type onto the screen the top characters on the double-character keys.

When you want to type in the graphics characters on the front of the keys, press and hold the SHIFT key and then tap the key to use the graphic character on the **right** side of the key.

For example **SHIFT + W** will produce a circle graphics character.

Press the SHIFT LOCK key to 'lock' the shift function on the keyboard. An arrow appears in the top-right corner of the screen to let you know that SHIFT LOCK is ON.

With this on, any key you press will act as if you are also holding down the SHIFT key. Press it again to turn SHIFT LOCK to OFF.

CRSR (CURSOR KEYS)

The two cursor control keys let you move the cursor around the screen. Use the ⇑ CRSR ⇓ key to move the cursor down, use it with the SHIFT key to move the cursor up. Use the ⇐CRSR⇒ key to move the cursor right, use it with the SHIFT key to move the cursor left.

You don't need to repeatedly tap the cursor key. Instead, you can hold it down to move the cursor to where you want it to go.

INST/DEL

The INST/DEL key is used for editing your program and other text on the screen. When you press the INST/DEL key by itself, it backspaces and deletes one character to the left of the cursor. When you press it with the SHIFT key it will insert a blank space to the right of the cursor.

The Insert functionality of the key is important when editing your programs. This is because whatever you type will overwrite what is already on the screen.

For example, I have a command that will PRINT out the word WORLD on screen. I want to actually PRINT out the words HELLO WORLD.   So, I use the CRSR keys to move my cursor over the letter W.

```
PRINT "WORLD"
```

I then press SHIFT+INST/DEL six times to insert enough spaces for my missing word.

```
PRINT "      WORLD"
```

Now I can type in the missing text.

```
PRINT "HELLO WORLD"
```

CLR/HOME

Pressed on its own, the CLR/HOME key will move the cursor back to its home position, the top-right corner of the screen. If you hold the SHIFT key and press the CLR/HOME key, it will clear the screen and move the cursor to its home position.

RESTORE

Hold down the RUN/STOP key and press the RESTORE key to restore your computer to its normal state. This will clear the screen, return it to its original colour and reset the video and sound chips.

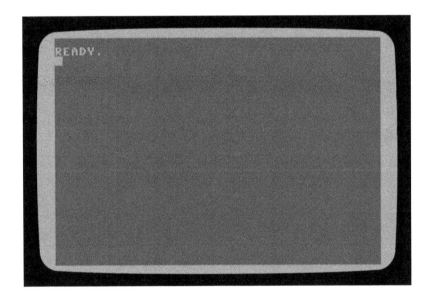

CTRL (CONTROL)

The Control key lets you perform special control functions on the computer. Use it with the number keys 1 to 8 to change the text colour to the colour written on that key. Press the CTRL key and the numbers 9 and 0 to produce reversed characters.

THEC64

Use this key with the SHIFT key to switch between the uppercase and lowercase display modes.

Use it with the numbers 1 to 8 to access the additional 8 colours.

When you want to type in the graphics characters on the front of the keys, press and hold the THEC64 key and then tap the key to use the graphic character on the **left** side of the key.

For example **THEC64 + W** will produce a sideways 'T' graphics character.

```
CTRL+1 = BLACK        C64+1 = ORANGE
CTRL+2 = WHITE
                      C64+3 = LIGHT RED
CTRL+4 = CYAN         C64+4 = GRAY 1
CTRL+5 = PURPLE       C64+5 = GRAY 2
CTRL+6 = GREEN        C64+6 = LIGHT GREEN
CTRL+7 = BLUE         C64+7 = LIGHT BLUE
CTRL+8 = YELLOW       C64+8 = GRAY 3
```

LESSON 1 GETTING STARTED

Connect your THEC64 and turn it on. By default, it will boot up into the Carousel mode, giving you a Graphical User Interface to a collection of pre-installed games. To begin your programming journey, you will need to access the Classic mode.

CLASSIC MODE

To access the Classic mode, use your joystick to open the **Device Settings** menu – click on the spanner icon.

Then select Switch to Classic Mode.

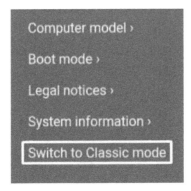

You will now be in THEC64's Classic Commodore 64 BASIC mode.

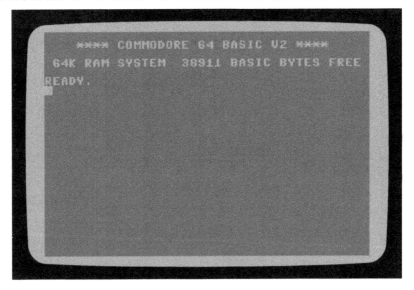

SET THE DEFAULT BOOT MODE

You can also set your THEC64 to automatically boot into Classic mode by default. To do this, access the **Device Settings** menu. Click the menu button on your joystick.

The menu appears at the bottom of the screen.

Select the **Options** item.

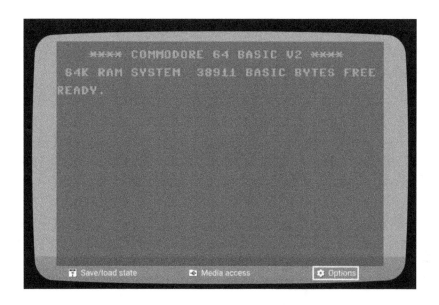

Select Device Settings > Boot Mode. Then select the Classic option.

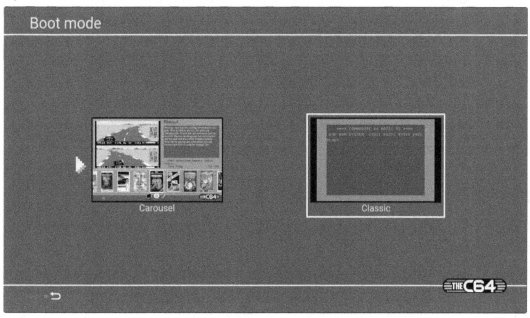

Click the menu button on the joystick to return to the Commodore 64 BASIC mode. Every time you start your THEC64, you will automatically boot into this mode.

BLANK VIRTUAL DISK

When you launch your THEC64 it automatically searches for an attached USB stick. If it finds one, it then searches for a compatible virtual disk file named THEC64-drive8.d64exists in the root directory of your USB stick. This file acts as if it is a floppy disk drive attached to your computer. You will need this up and running in order to save and load the programs you create during this course.

STEP 1: PREPARE YOUR USB

You will need a USB drive that you are happy to completely erase of any existing files. Choose a USB stick that is 32GB or less in size. You will need to use an existing computer to format the USB drive using the FAT32 (or FAT) format with Master Boot Record (MBR). The steps for doing this vary depending on the type and version of your computer's operating system. I suggest you follow the steps outlined in Appendix B of THEC64 User Manual, which can be downloaded for free at:

https://retrogames.biz/thec64/support/manuals-thec64

STEP 2: INITIALISE THE USB

Make sure your THEC64 is turned off. Insert your formatted USB stick and turn it on.

Check your USB now has a blank virtual disk. Click the **Menu** button on your joystick and select the **Media access** option.

You will see that your blank virtual disk is listed. Notice that the virtual disk is also listed as being 'inserted' into the computers virtual disk drive.

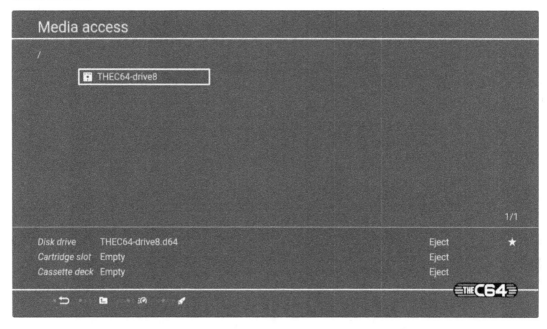

Exit the menu. You are ready to begin your Commodore 64 coding journey on your THEC64.

LESSON 2 YOUR FIRST PROGRAM

We are going to write your very first Commodore 64 BASIC program, save it to your virtual disk and then list the contents of your virtual disk to see if everything worked as expected.

ENTER YOUR FIRST PROGRAM

Make sure you are in Classic mode.

Type in the following BASIC computer code exactly as it is written below. Be sure to press the RETURN key after every line.

```
10 PRINT "HELLO WORLD"
20 GOTO 10
```

Every time you type a line of BASIC code and hit the RETURN key; the computer places it into the short-term memory of the computer.

Let's examine what each part of this program does.

Firstly, you will notice that each line begins with a line number. This tells the computer in what order to run each line of code. Traditionally, we increment the line numbers by 10. This means that if we find we need to insert a few extra lines of code, we have another 9 number to use to add these extra commands.

The program is very simple. The first line tells the computer to PRINT the words HELLO WORLD to the screen. The second line tells the computer to go to line 10. The computer will loop back to the first command to PRINT the text to screen.

Now you are ready to run your first program. To run a program that is loaded in the computer's memory we use the BASIC command **RUN**. Type the word RUN and hit RETURN.

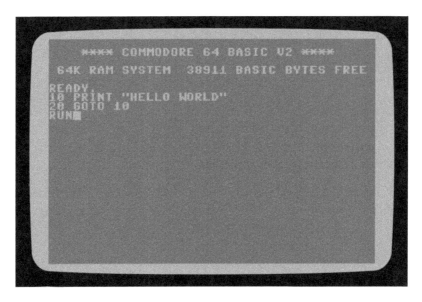

You will see a column of text run down the screen as your program repeatedly PRINTs the words HELLO WORLD on the screen. We wrote our program to cause what is known as an *infinite loop*. The computer will simply keep on looping through our code with no way to know how to stop.

Press the RUN/STOP key to force your program to stop.

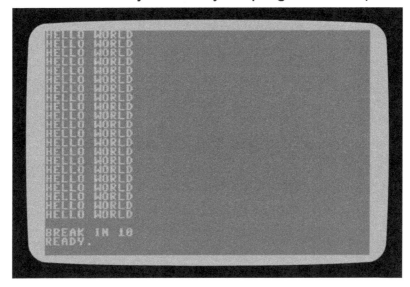

Notice how the computer tells you which line you in your code that the computer cancelled the programming running.

LIST YOUR PROGRAM

The program is sitting in the computer's short-term memory. You can list the code of any program that is in memory by using the LIST command. Type in LIST and press the RETURN key.

Your program will display on the screen.

EDIT YOUR PROGRAM

Let's try a couple of ways that we can edit a program listing. Firstly, let's add a new line of code between lines 10 and 20. Type in a new line 15 and tell the computer to PRINT some text of your choice.

For example:

```
15 PRINT "HELLO PERTH!!!"
```

Now, type the LIST command and press the RETURN key to list the edited computer program. [Note, from now on I will not remind you to press the RETURN key when you want to run a command.]

Notice that even though we typed line 15 in last, when we list the full program the computer lists it in the order it will execute the code ('execute' is just the way computer programmers refer to it when a computer runs a program).

Next, we will edit an existing line of code to change it. I want to change line 10 to say hello to me.   Theoretically we could just type in a new line of code and if we give it the line number 10, it will replace what was already in line number 10.

Instead, we can use the LIST command to PRINT out our program on the screen and then use our cursor keys to move our cursor to the line and change it there.

Let's do it. Use your cursor keys to change line number 10 to say HELLO [YOUR NAME]. E.g.

```
10 PRINT "HELLO RICHARD"
```

When you press the RETURN key after editing the line of code, it will replace the code currently in memory for line 10 with the edited version you just typed in.

```
10 PRINT "HELLO RICHARD"
15 PRINT "HELLO PERTH!!!"
20 GOTO 10
READY.
```

Use the cursor keys to move back down the page past the READY prompt and use the RUN command to execute your newly edited program.

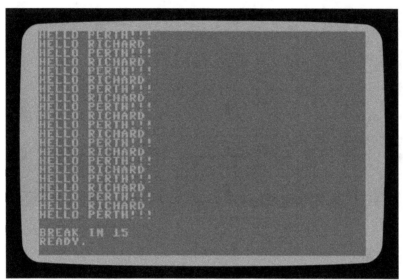

SAVE YOUR PROGRAM TO DISK

Your program currently sits in the computer's short-term memory, known as Random Access Memory or RAM. If you turn off your computer, you will lose everything in the RAM. To keep a copy of your program long term, you will need to save it to the Virtual Disk.

To save your computer program to disk we use the SAVE command in the following format: SAVE "[FILE-NAME]",8. This will save your program as the filename you type between the quotation marks.

The ,8 part of the command tells the computer to save it to the disk drive. Type in a SAVE command to store your program.

```
SAVE "HELLO-WORLD",8
```

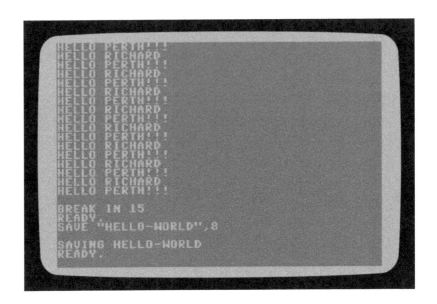

LOAD YOUR PROGRAM FROM DISK

Turn your computer off (hold down the power button for 2 seconds) and then turn it back on again to wipe out program from RAM.

You can check that your program is no longer in memory by typing the LIST command once you restart your computer.

If you know the file name of the program you want to load, you can load it straight away. However, let's look at how you can view the list of files on your virtual disk. We will use the LOAD command to load something into the computer's RAM. We use the $ symbol to specify we want to load the contents of the disk directory into memory.

Type in the following commands:

```
LOAD "$",8
LIST
```

You will see all the files that have been saved on this disk.

To load your program, type in the load command using the file name you used to save it with.

```
LOAD "HELLO-WORLD",8
```

You can now LIST and RUN your code again.

The LOAD command replaces whatever is currently within the computer's RAM. This means that if you now re-run the directory load command, it will replace your code with the directory listing. Try it.

```
LOAD "$",8
RUN
```

The computer will display a Syntax Error. This means that whatever is currently in memory cannot be run as a BASIC language computer program. Go ahead and re-load your program and check that it does indeed now run correctly.

LESSON 3 BUILDING BLOCKS

In this chapter we will look at the basic building blocks of coding the Commodore 64 in BASIC. Don't be tempted to skip this section. It lays a solid foundation for the rest of the course.

DISPLAY NUMBERS AND TEXT

Remember how we used the SHIFT + CLR/HOME key combination to clear the screen and send the cursor to the home position? You can do the exact same thing by PRINTing the matching character code to the screen. (Don't worry about character codes yet, just try out the following exercise).

The character code for to clear the screen is 157. We can use the PRINT CHR$(147) command to PRINT this character code to the screen. However, computers need you to be exactly correct when you type in commands and if you get it even just slightly wrong, it will display some kind of error message.

For example, if you type in PRINT CHRS(147) or PRNT CHR$(147) the computer will display an error message. Try it and see what happens.

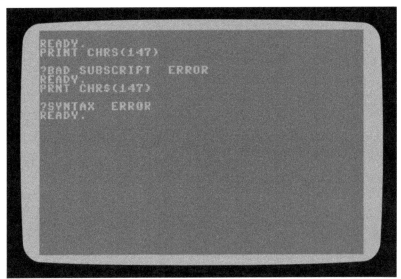

DISPLAY A NUMBER

Clear the screen and type the following command to display a number.

```
PRINT 7
```

Try this with other numbers.

DISPLAY SOME TEXT

When you want to display text, called a **String** in programming languages, you use the PRINT command and type the text you want to appear inside quotation marks. For example:

```
PRINT "COMMODORE 64"
```

Try it with other strings. You can use any characters on the keyboard to PRINT.

USING VARIABLES

So far, we have displayed numbers and strings using static values. Let's have a look at what is called **Variables**.

Clear the screen and type in the following command.

```
PRINT AGE
```

The result might surprise you. Instead of displaying the word AGE, the computer displayed the number 0. Now type in this command:

```
PRINT "AGE"
```

This time the computer responded as you might have originally expected. When you use a word without the surrounding quotation marks, the computer thinks you are referring to a variable called AGE. A variable is a label for a particular slot in its memory. When you typed in the command without quotation marks, the computer searched its memory for a slot labelled AGE and when it couldn't find it, it created it and assigned an initial value of 0.

We use the command LET to assign a value to a variable. Let's assign a value to our variable AGE.

```
LET AGE=43
```

Now type the command to display the variable AGE to screen. When you use a word without quotation marks it always refers to a variable that points to a numeric value.

What if we want to have a variable that points to a string value? In that case we use a word that ends with the $ symbol. For example, we can use the variable CITY$ to hold the string value of a city.

Assign a string value to the variable CITY$.

```
LET CITY$="PERTH"
```

Now type the command to display the variable CITY to screen.

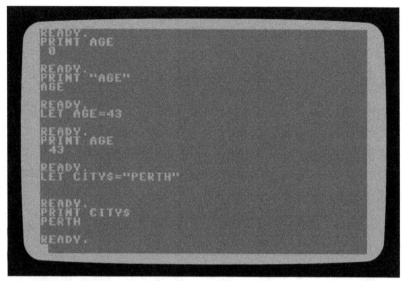

You can change the value of a variable as many times as you like. Let's change the value of CITY$.

```
LET CITY$="LOS ANGELES"
```

Experiment with assigning and displaying some numeric and string variables.

COLOURS

The Commodore 64 can display 16 colours, all of which can be accessed from the keyboard. In this section you will learn some ways of displaying colour on the screen.

By default, the Commodore 64's display is blue with a light blue border. Let's go ahead and change the display to black instead, type in:

```
POKE 53280,0:POKE 53281,0
```

(You will find out how these commands work in a later lesson.)

CHANGE COLOURS USING THE KEYBOARD

If you look at the Keyboard you will see 8 colours PRINTed on the front of the number keys 1 to 8. You can change the current text colour by holding the CTRL key and tapping one of these number keys. Another 8 colours can be accessed by holding the THEC64 key and tapping one of the number keys.

Go ahead and experiment with changing text colours using the keyboard.

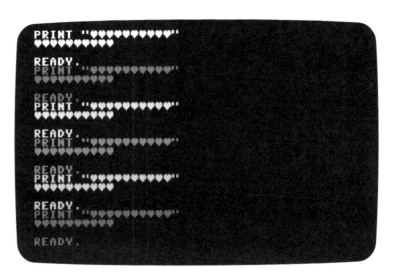

(You can access the heart character using SHIFT + S.)

CHANGE COLOURS USING CONTROL SYMBOLS

Instead of using the keyboard, you can use control symbols in a string variable to change the colours. This is useful because the colour doesn't change until the actual string is instructed to PRINT, which can be useful when writing your own programs.

Typing in colour control symbols is easy, you do it exactly the same way that you used to change the colours using the keyboard. However, because we are declaring a string variable using the LET command, a graphic symbol is inserted into the string.

Let's declare a string called C$ and make it PRINT out a purple string.

```
LET C$="[CTRL+5] THEC64 ROCKS!"
```

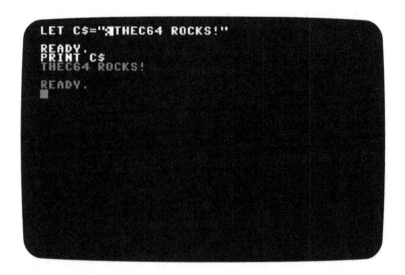

Although using colour control symbols is easy to type in using the keyboard, it is much harder to do so if we are trying to copy in the code from a computer program listing. Instead, we can use a third way.

CHANGE COLOURS USING CHARACTER CODES

The Commodore 64 uses a set of codes called American Standard Code for Information Interchange or ASCII to represent all of the characters that can be PRINTed to the screen. For example, the capital letter A is represented by the ASCII code 65, the capital letter B by 66 and so on. There are ASCII codes also for operations such as moving the cursor, creating a new line and changing the text colour.

(The full set of ASCII codes used in the Commodore 64 are included in the Appendices at the back of this book.)

In Commodore BASIC you use the CHR$ command to produce the character or operation of an ASCII code.

ASCII Colour Codes

Colour	ASCII Code	Colour	ASCII Code
Black	144	Orange	129
White	5	Brown	149
Red	28	Light Red	150
Cyan	159	Dark Gray	151
Purple	156	Medium Gray	152
Green	30	Light Green	153
Blue	31	Light Blue	154
Yellow	158	Light Gray	155
Reverse On	18	Reverse Off	146

```
PRINT CHR$(159); "1234567890"
1234567890

READY.
PRINT CHR$(5); "●0●0●0●0●0●0"
●0●0●0●0●0●0

READY.
PRINT CHR$(158); "************"
************

READY.
```

You can also use the CHR$ command and ASCII codes when defining string variables. To do this you can use what is called 'String Concatenation', that is, joining more than one string or ASCII code command together into a single string variable.

For example, we want to declare a string variable A$, set the colour to White, display some text, change the colour to Green and then display some more text.

```
LET A$ = CHR$(5)+"ONE " +CHR$(30)+"TWO"
```

Then PRINT the A$ variable to display the text and colour codes.

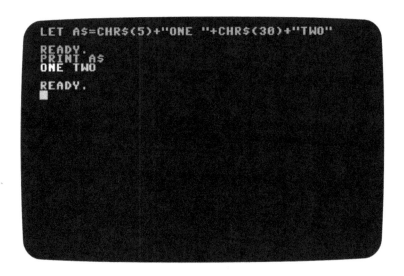

```
LET A$=CHR$(5)+"ONE "+CHR$(30)+"TWO"

READY.
PRINT A$
ONE TWO

READY.
```

CALCULATIONS

You can use BASIC code to perform a wide variety of mathematical calculations.

BASIC CALCULATIONS

The four basic mathematics calculations have matching symbols in much the same way that symbols are used on a calculator.

+ Add
- Subtract
* Multiply
/ Divide

Use the PRINT command to perform some basic maths calculations and display the result on the screen.

```
PRINT 165+34
 199

READY.
PRINT 65-12
 53

READY.
PRINT 6*12
 72

READY.
PRINT 58/4.5
 12.8888889

READY.
■
```

ADVANCED CALCULATIONS

You can use in-built mathematical functions to calculate the exponents and square roots of numbers. Exponential numbers are a number multiplied by itself a specified number of times. For example, 2^3 is the same as doing 2x2x2 which equals 8. To do an exponential calculation on the Commodore 64, you use the up-arrow character. So, 2^3 is entered as 2↑3.

There isn't a character used to represent the square root calculation, instead we use the SQR command, for example SQR(2) to calculate the square root of 2.

```
PRINT 4↑3
 64

READY.
PRINT 6↑4
 1296

READY.
PRINT SQR(2)
 1.41421356

READY.
PRINT SQR(16)
 4

READY.
```

SEQUENCING CALCULATIONS

You can chain together a number of calculation steps into a single
calculation. Say you want to add to numbers together and divide the
result by 2.   You might think the order you type the numbers in
should not make a difference because 6+2 is the same as 2+6.
However, you will see something you might not expect when you try
this on your computer.

```
PRINT 6+2/2
 7
READY.
PRINT 2+6/2
 5
READY.
PRINT (6+2)/2
 4
READY.
PRINT (2+6)/2
 4
READY.
■
```

Your computer will not necessarily process your calculation in the order you type it in. Computers use what is called the BIMDAS order of mathematical operations. BIMDAS represents the following order that is used:

1. **B**rackets
2. **I**ndices
3. **M**ultiplication and **D**ivision
4. **A**ddition and **S**ubtraction

In our example above, we wanted the computer to add the first two numbers together first before dividing that result by the third number. However, by following the rules of BIMDAS the computer performs the division first and then performs the addition second. You can see that neither of the first two calculations produced the result we were looking for. To change the order, we needed to use brackets to define which part of the calculation to perform first.

LIMITS FOR NUMBERS

The Commodore 64 has two kinds of limits when it comes to its numbers, size and accuracy.

In terms of size, numbers that have a decimal point you can have any number between 1x1038 (1 followed by 38 zeros) to -1x10^{38} (-1 followed by 38 zeros). Whole numbers (also called integers) can be within the range of 32,767 to -32,768.

In terms of accuracy, although you can store a number with a decimal point in a very large range (size), the computer only stores the first nine digits, the rest it sets to zero. For whole numbers, the computer stores these with complete accuracy.

For very large numbers, you will notice that the computer will display these in a strange format that uses the letter E. Try the following command:

```
PRINT 1000000000000
```

It will PRINT 1E+12 on the screen. The E stands for 'exponent' and is a shorthand way of displaying 1x10^{12} or 1 followed by 12 zeros.

Try displaying and executing some large number calculations of your own. What do you think the ?OVERFLOW ERROR means?

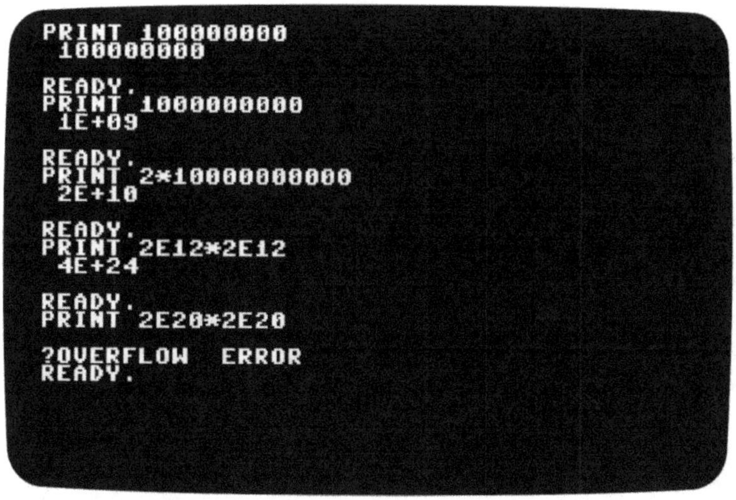

```
PRINT 100000000
 100000000

READY.
PRINT 1000000000
 1E+09

READY.
PRINT 2*10000000000
 2E+10

READY.
PRINT 2E12*2E12
 4E+24

READY.
PRINT 2E20*2E20

?OVERFLOW  ERROR
READY.
```

DISPLAYING LISTINGS

So that we have a program to list, type the following code into your
Commodore 64. Then RUN the program.

```
10 REM SCREEN DISPLAY
20 PRINT TAB(8); "*************"
30 PRINT TAB(8); "*"; TAB(19); "*"
40 PRINT TAB(8); "*"; TAB(12); "MATH"; TAB(19); "*"
50 PRINT TAB(8); "*"; TAB(19); "*"
60 PRINT TAB(8); "*"; TAB(11); "8/2="; 8/2; TAB(19); "*"
70 PRINT TAB(8); "*"; TAB(19); "*"
80 PRINT TAB(8); "*************"
```

```
LIST
10 REM SCREEN DISPLAY
20 PRINT TAB(8); "***********"
30 PRINT TAB(8); "*"; TAB(19); "*"
40 PRINT TAB(8); "*"; TAB(12); "MATH"; T
AB(19); "*"
50 PRINT TAB(8); "*"; TAB(19); "*"
60 PRINT TAB(8); "*"; TAB(11); "8/2="; 8
/2; TAB(19); "*"
70 PRINT TAB(8); "*"; TAB(19); "*"
80 PRINT TAB(8); "***********"
READY.
RUN
        ***********
        *         *
        *   MATH  *
        *         *
        *  8/2= 4 *
        *         *
        ***********
READY.
■
```

Let's look at what the above code does.

In line 10, the code REM stands for REMark, the computer doesn't do anything with this line. These are designed to let you add comments into your programs to help you label your code to help you identify and understand sections of your program.

Lines 20 to 80 PRINT * symbols in a frame around some text and a calculation. These lines use the TAB command to position the symbols and text around the screen at the correct positions. PRINT TAB(8) means that the computer will start the display at column 8 on the screen instead of the left-hand edge. The semi-colon symbol is used to chain together a group of items to display when you want to show them all on the same line.

Go ahead and save your program to disk.

```
SAVE "MATH",8
```

Let's explore the LIST command. We already know that typing the command by itself will list out the entire program. However, there are some neat little tricks that will become very useful when you begin entering very large program listings.

You can list a single line by tying the LIST command followed by the line number, for example, LIST 10.

You can look at a range of lines, say lines 40 to 50 by using LIST 40-50. Look at the first 30 lines with LIST -30 or all the lines from 70 until the end of the program with LIST 70-.

```
LIST 10
10 REM SCREEN DISPLAY
READY.
LIST 40-50

40 PRINT TAB(8); "*"; TAB(12); "MATH"; T
AB(19); "*"
50 PRINT TAB(8); "*"; TAB(19); "*"

READY.
LIST -30

10 REM SCREEN DISPLAY
20 PRINT TAB(8); "*************"
30 PRINT TAB(8); "*"; TAB(19); "*"

READY.
LIST 70-

70 PRINT TAB(8); "*"; TAB(19); "*"
80 PRINT TAB(8); "*************"
READY.
```

If you have a very long program and you want to scroll through the listing while looking for a particular section of code, just use the LIST command on its own. You will notice that the code scrolls very fast. However, you can slow down the list scrolling by holding down the CTRL key. When you see the section you want, hit the STOP key to abort, or BREAK, the listing. You can then LIST the specific line or range of lines you were looking for.

CORRECTING MISTAKES

38

Mistakes are an unavoidable part of computer programming. Sometimes you need to correct a simple mistyped line, maybe you want to change something already in the program or you want to add in a line you forgot to when you first keyed in your code.

Say we want to change our Math screen display program from earlier. Instead of calculating 8/2 we want to calculate 8*2. We could simply retype line 60 in and replace it with our new line, but because we only want to change to characters in the line, we can use our cursor control keys to edit the line instead.

You could LIST the entire program code listing, but because we know which line we want to edit, we will just list line 60. Then we use the cursor control keys, along with the SHIFT key to move our cursor over the first / symbol. Then we can type over that with the * symbol instead. (If you ever need to edit a line that needs more room for your changes you will need to use the INSRT key to add in the required number of spaces before typing in your change.)

Once you have made the changes, press the RETURN key to save your changes.

```
LIST 60
60 PRINT TAB(8); "*"; TAB(11); "8*2="; 8
*2; TAB(19); "*"
READY.
```

Often you will want to add in a line into your code. For example, we want to add in a line to clear the screen before anything is PRINTed to the screen. You don't need to edit any line numbers to do this. This is why we use multiples of 10 for our line numbers, it makes adding in new lines much easier.

Try:

```
5 PRINT CHR$(147)
```

ERROR MESSAGES

Mistakes or errors in code are called bugs and the processes of troubleshooting and fixing these errors is called debugging. The Commodore 64 has a range of helpful error messages to help you track down and fix these bugs in your code.

Try the following typing in and RUNning the following small programs that each contain an error. You should be able to see which line the error happens on.

```
10 FOR X=60 TO 100
20 PRINT 2↑X,3↑X
30 NEXT X
```

```
10 FOR X=0 TO 20
20 INPUT B
30 PRINT B/X
40 NEXT X
```

```
10 INPUT "ENTER A NUMBER ";A
20 FOR F=1 TO 12
30 PRINT TAB(9);F;"*";A;"=";F*A
40 NEXT G
```

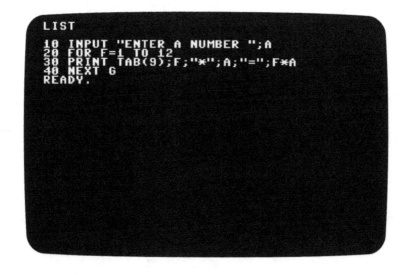

LESSON 4 INPUT AND OUTPUT

Remember how we assigned values to string and numeric variables? Well, instead of setting these within the code itself, we can get the user to enter a value. We use the INPUT command to interrupt the running, or execution, of a program, ask the user a question and wait for the user to type in a response. This is then assigned to either a numeric or string variable. Try the following code.

```
10  PRINT CHR$(147)
20  INPUT "WHAT IS YOUR NAME";NAME$
30  INPUT "WHAT IS YOUR AGE";AGE
40  PRINT CHR$(147)
50  PRINT "HELLO ";NAME$
60  PRINT "ARE YOU REALLY";AGE;"YEAR'S OLD?"
```

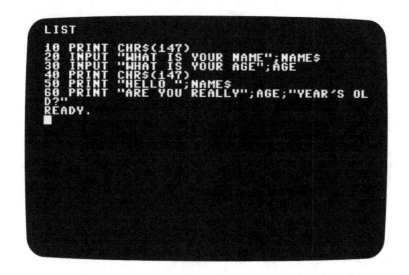

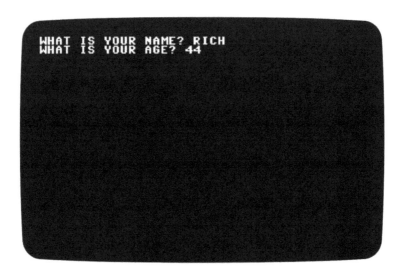

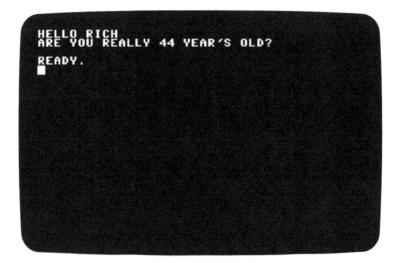

FORMATTING YOUR OUTPUT

There are a few handy built-in ways to format and space out the output of your programs. Try the following program.

```
10 PRINT CHR$(147)
```

```
20  PRINT "LENGTH CONVERSION PROGRAM"
30  PRINT : INPUT "HOW MANY INCHES";I
40  PRINT : PRINT I;" INCHES = "; I*2.54; "CENTIMETERS"
```

```
LENGTH CONVERSION
HOW MANY INCHES? 5
 5  INCHES =  12.7 CENTIMETERS
READY.
```

RUN this program. Let's look at a couple of things going on with the formatting. Firstly, we used an extra PRINT command followed by a colon to PRINT in an extra blank line on lines 30 and 40. This is a good way to help space out and group together parts of your program output. Secondly, one line 40 we use the semi-colon symbol to PRINT all of the output right next to each other. There are two other ways we can format the output.

Change the semi-colons in line 40 to commas instead (also remove the spaces within the quotation marks). RUN the program and see how this has changed the output.

```
40  PRINT : PRINT I,"INCHES=",I*2.54,"CENTIMETERS"
```

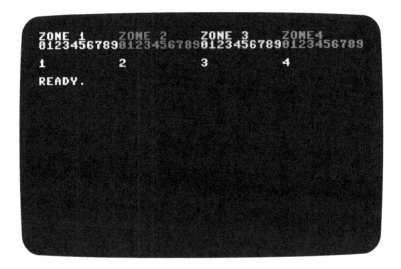

```
LENGTH CONVERSION
HOW MANY INCHES? 5
 5           INCHES=     12.7      CENTIMETER
S
READY.
```

You can see that using commas has spaced out the output across the screen. The Commodore 64 display is 40 characters wide. It is divided into four invisible zones of 10 characters wide each. When you use a comma within a PRINT statement, it causes the output to be displayed starting in the next zone.

```
ZONE 1      ZONE 2      ZONE 3      ZONE4
0123456789012345678901234567890123456789
1           2           3           4
READY.
```

The last method of formatting your program output we have already experimented with – TABs. When you PRINT using a TAB statement, it will begin the next part of the display at the number of spaces along that you specify in the TAB statement. For example, PRINT TAB(12) will begin displaying at column 12, or 12 spaces in.

```
PRINT TAB(12); "TAB(12)"
            TAB(12)

READY.
PRINT TAB(25); "TAB(25)"
                        TAB(25)

READY.
PRINT TAB(4); "TAB(4)"
     TAB(4)

READY.
```

LESSON 5 LOOPS

Many programs that you write will need to perform part of its functionality more than once. This where programming loops come in.

GOTO LOOPS

We have already encountered the first way we can construct loops, using the GOTO statement. GOTO simply directs the computer to go to a particular line of your code. Try the following program (the first two lines just set up the colours):

```
10 POKE 53280,5; POKE 53281,6
20 PRINT CHR$(5)
30 PRINT CHR$(147)
40 LET X=1
50 PRINT X,X+X,X*X
60 LET X=X+1
70 GOTO 50
```

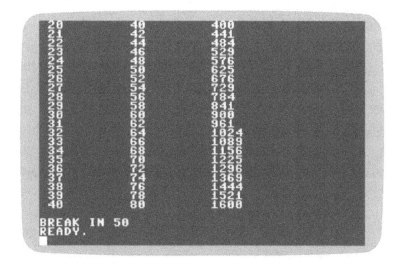

Using a GOTO loop has one big disadvantage; it is never ending. We call them infinite loops. The only way to stop this kind of loop is to press the STOP key and cancel the program execution.

FOR … NEXT LOOPS

One solution to endless loops is to use FOR … NEXT loops.   Edit the previous program to match the one below so that it uses a FOR … NEXT loop in the place of the GOTO loop.

```
10 POKE 53280,5; POKE 53281,6
20 PRINT CHR$(5)
30 PRINT CHR$(147)
40 FOR X=1 TO 20
50 PRINT X,X+X,X*X
60 NEXT X
```

You can see the loop run from lines 50 to 60. A FOR … NEXT loop begins with the FOR statement. In this case, it sets the numeric variable X to equal 1 and lets the computer know that the values of X will run from 1 to 20. Line 50 contains the loop code. In our case it is just a single line of output, but there could be many lines of code in the body of the loop. Finally, the loop finishes with the NEXT X statement.   This tells the computer to increment X, or add 1 to X, and then go back up to the top of the loop body and process the code again. When X is set to 20, it will run through the loop one last time before continuing on through your code, in our case it is the end of program and so it finishes back to the READY prompt.

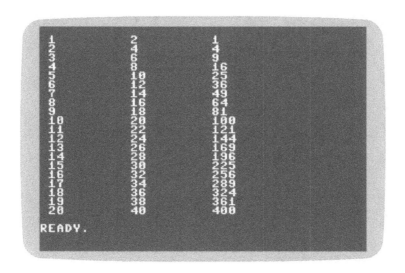

```
1      2       1
2      4       4
3      6       9
4      8       16
5      10      25
6      12      36
7      14      49
8      16      64
9      18      81
10     20      100
11     22      121
12     24      144
13     26      169
14     28      196
15     30      225
16     32      256
17     34      289
18     36      324
19     38      361
20     40      400
READY.
```

You can also use the INPUT statement to get data from the user in the middle of a FOR … NEXT loop. The computer will pause in the loop and wait for a user response before continuing processing the loop. In this next example we will type in a program that converts miles to kilometres and uses a loop to allow the user to do the conversion 5 times before finishing.

```
10 FOR X=1 TO 5
20 PRINT CHR$(147)
30 PRINT : PRINT TAB(10);"DISTANCE CONVERSION"
40 POKE 214,12 : PRINT : POKE 211,4
50 INPUT "ENTER YOUR DISTANCE IN MILES";M
60 POKE 214,18 : PRINT : POKE 211,8
70 PRINT M;"MILES = ";M*1.61;"KMS"
80 FOR A=1 TO 3000 : NEXT A
90 NEXT X
```

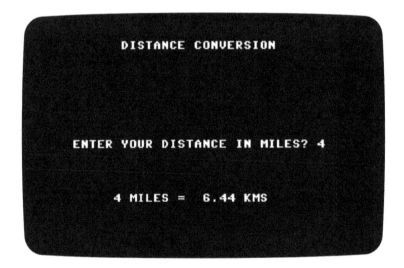

```
LIST

10 FOR X=1 TO 5
20 PRINT CHR$(147)
30 PRINT : PRINT TAB(10);"DISTANCE CONVE
RSION"
40 POKE 214,12 : PRINT : POKE 211,4
50 INPUT "ENTER YOUR DISTANCE IN MILES";
M
60 POKE 214,18 : PRINT : POKE 211,8
70 PRINT M;"MILES = ";M*1.61;"KMS"
80 FOR A=1 TO 3000 : NEXT A
90 NEXT X
READY.
```

```
                DISTANCE CONVERSION




         ENTER YOUR DISTANCE IN MILES? 4



           4 MILES =   6.44 KMS
```

You will notice that we have put in a one-line loop within our main program loop. When we put one loop inside another like this it is called 'nesting' loops. When you nest loops, you have to make sure that there is a NEXT for every FOR in your code.

On line 80 our nested loop looks like this:

```
80 FOR A=1 TO 3000 : NEXT A
```

This single line will loop over itself 3000 times before continuing on with the program execution. This is a neat little way to slow your program down if you need to. In our case, we want the computer to pause for about 3 seconds so that the user can ready the results of their calculation before clearing the screen for the next calculation.

(For a bonus challenge, what do you think lines 40 and 60 do? Try play with the values after the comma to see what happens. You will find out more about the POKE statement later in this course.)

LESSON 6 DECISIONS

Your Commodore 64 uses the IF ... THEN statement to make decisions. You use this statement in your code when you want the computer to ask the question, "IF [a condition is true] THEN [do something]". For example, we are going to write a simple maths quiz game. In it we will need to get the computer to ask the question, "IF [the answer is correct] THEN [show the correct message]". We will use a new command called RND to generate a random number.

```
10  PRINT CHR$(147);CHR$(31):POKE 53280,6:POKE 53281,1
20  FOR Y=1 TO 10
30  FOR X=1 TO 40
40  PRINT "?";
50  NEXT X : NEXT Y
60  X=INT(RND(0)*10) : Y=INT(RND(0)*10)
70  POKE 214,12 : PRINT : POKE 211,15
80  PRINT "                            "
90  POKE 214,12 : PRINT : POKE 211,15
100 PRINT CHR$(31);X;"+";Y;"=";:INPUT A
110 IF A=X+Y THEN 150
120 POKE 214,12 : PRINT : POKE 211,15
130 PRINT CHR$(28);"INCORRECT            "
140 FOR T=1 TO 500:NEXT T: GOTO 70
150 POKE 214,12 : PRINT : POKE 211,15
160 PRINT CHR$(30); "CORRECT            "
170 FOR T=1 TO 500:NEXT T: GOTO 60
```

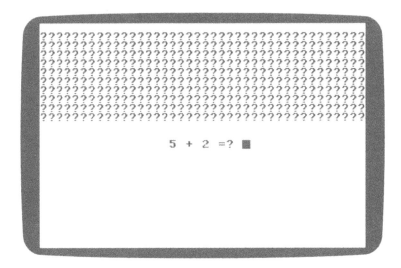

```
LIST

10 PRINT CHR$(147);CHR$(31):POKE 53280,6
:POKE 53281,1
20 FOR Y=1 TO 10
30 FOR X=1 TO 40
40 PRINT "?";
50 NEXT X : NEXT Y
60 X=INT(RND(0)*10) : Y=INT(RND(0)*10)
70 POKE 214,12 : PRINT : POKE 211,15
80 PRINT "
"
90 POKE 214,12 : PRINT : POKE 211,15
100 PRINT CHR$(31);X;"+";Y;"=";:INPUT A
110 IF A=X+Y THEN 150
120 POKE 214,12 : PRINT : POKE 211,15
130 PRINT CHR$(28);"INCORRECT
"
140 FOR T=1 TO 500:NEXT T: GOTO 70
150 POKE 214,12 : PRINT : POKE 211,15
160 PRINT CHR$(30);"CORRECT
"
170 FOR T=1 TO 500:NEXT T: GOTO 60
READY.
```

Let's examine this program in a bit of detail. Lines 10 to 40 set up the look and feel of the program, the colours and the rows of question marks. Can you see how we used two nested loops (X and Y) to PRINT 12 rows of 40 question marks?

Line 60 uses two new BASIC commands. The RND(0)*10 command generates a random number between 0 and 9. However, this includes numbers with many decimal places (e.g. 6.32815421). We just want whole numbers, so we use the INT, or Integer, command. INT rounds downward to the nearest whole number. So, by combining these two commands we get two random numbers between 0 and 9.

We use the POKE commands to position the display at the exact same position on the screen for every bit of output from our program (see lines 70, 90, 120 and 150). Each new bit of output overwrites what was already there.

On line 100 we display the question and use the INPUT command to get the answer from the user.

The on line 110 we use the IF … THEN decision command. You can see that we check if their answer, variable A, is equal to the question X+Y. If it is, we send the computer to line 150, if it is not correct the computer simply continues running to the next line.

So, if the answer is correct, we jump down to line 150. Line 150 positions the display. Line 160 PRINTs a 'correct' message. Line 170 pauses briefly and then send the computer back to line 60 to generate and display a new question.

If the answer is incorrect, the computer ignores the IF … THEN statement and simply continues on to the next line, line 120. Line 120 positions the display. Line 130 PRINTs an 'incorrect' message. Line 140 pauses briefly and then send the computer back to line 70 to re-display the current question and get a new answer from the user.

You can see that a powerful set of functionality can be created by using a combination of FOR … NEXT, IF … THEN and GOTO loops.

IF … THEN Conditions

These symbols specify what kind of comparison the computer calculates when you use an IF … THEN statement.

=	Is equal to	<>	Is not equal to
>	Is greater than	<	Is less than
>=	Is greater than or equal to	<=	Is less than or equal to

LESSON 7 POKE AND PEEK

On some computers, a great deal of memory space is given over to the BASIC command interpreter so that they have a large vocabulary of commands to choose from. Often these machines have commands to create graphics and sound, commands like COLOR, DRAW and SOUND. However, the Commodore 64's BASIC vocabulary is smaller so that it uses less memory leaving more memory available for your own program code. Instead, the Commodore 64 provides two general-purpose commands that will enable you to carry out these and other more advanced functionality – POKE and PEEK.

The command POKE allows you to put a number directly into a specific location of the computer's memory. PEEK does the opposite; it allows you to read the value of a specific location in RAM.

CHANGE COLOURS WITH POKE

RAM, or Random Access Memory, is the part of the computer that temporarily stores all of the information that it needs right now. RAM is segmented into individually locatable areas and each area is given an individual numeric address. Using the POKE and PEEK commands, you can set and fetch the value of each memory location by using its address.

The Commodore 64 'knows' what colours to display in the border and background sections of the screen by 'looking' at what values are currently stored in two memory locations. Memory location 53280 holds the border colour and location 53281 holds the background colour. Try the following program to manipulate the border and background colours using the POKE command.

```
10 PRINT CHR$(147)
20 FOR I=0 TO 15
```

```
30 POKE 53280,I : POKE 53281,I
40 FOR T=1 TO 1000 : NEXT T
50 NEXT I
```

```
LIST
10 PRINT CHR$(147)
20 FOR I=0 TO 15
30 POKE 53280,I : POKE 53281,I
40 FOR T=1 TO 1000 : NEXT T
50 NEXT I
READY.
```

We use a FOR ... NEXT loop to cycle through the 16 colours (values 0 to 15). For each colour value, we use the POKE command to set the value of the two memory locations controlling the border and background colours.

CONTROL THE CURSOR WITH POKE

Two other useful memory locations we can explore are those that control the position of the cursor on the screen. The Commodore 64 screen is divided into 40 rows (rows 0 to 39) each with 25 columns (columns 0 to 24). Any possible position on screen can be controlled by setting the values for the row and column. The column position is controlled by memory location 211 and the row position by location 214. Try this program.

```
10 PRINT CHR$(147)
20 INPUT "(0-39) ROW=";R
30 INPUT "(0-24) COL=";C
40 PRINT CHR$(147)
50 POKE 211,R : POKE 214,C
60 PRINT "X"
```

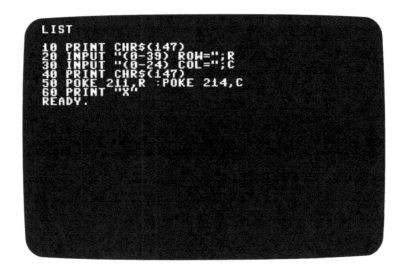

HAVING A PEEK AT MEMORY

Type in the following command to display the value of the memory location that controls the cursor colour:

```
PRINT PEEK(646)
```

(Bonus challenge: type a command to change the colour of the cursor using POKE.)

The PEEK command is often used to fetch the value of a memory location, modifying it in some way and then placing (POKEing) it back into memory.

LESSON 8 CHARACTER GRAPHICS

We saw earlier that characters and control keys on the keyboard are represented by ASCII numbers within the computer. The character set used on Commodore Business Machines (including the PET, C16, C64, C128, CBM-II, Plus/4 and VIC-20) is called PETSCII. You can use the ASCII codes to display characters to screen without using the keyboard to enter them into your program. Enter this short program that uses the ASCII codes to PRINT the character set of the Commodore 64 to the screen.

```
10 PRINT CHR$(147)
20 FOR C=33 TO 127
30 PRINT CHR$(C);" ";
40 NEXT C
50 FOR C=161 TO 255
60 PRINT CHR$(C);" ";
70 NEXT C
```

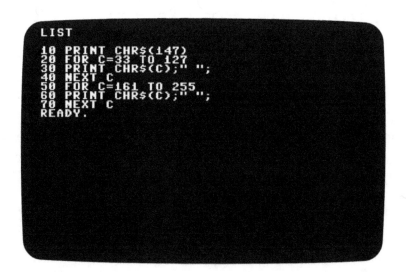

We use two loops so that we can easily skip over the ASCII codes from 128 to 160, which are largely control codes.

DESIGNING CHARACTER GRAPHICS

You can create quite complex graphics using just the set of characters that come in built with the Commodore 64. In fact, there is a whole branch of computer-based art called PETSCII Art. Let's create some of our own PETSCII art on your own computer.

THE WALL

This little program uses just two characters to build up a wall on the screen. One character looks like a short letter T (ASCII code 178) and the other an upside version of this character (ASCII code 177). The program will set some colours and then alternately PRINT each character in turn across the screen.

```
10 PRINT CHR$(147) : POKE 53280,12 : POKE 53281,2
20 PRINT CHR$(5); : C=1
30 FOR K=1 TO 20 : FOR D=1 TO 40
40 IF C=1 THEN PRINT CHR$(178); : GOTO 60
```

```
50 PRINT CHR$(177);
60 C=1-C : NEXT D
70 C=1-C : NEXT K
```

```
LIST
10 PRINT CHR$(147) : POKE 53280,12 : POK
E 53281,2
20 PRINT CHR$(5) : C=1
30 FOR K=1 TO 20 : FOR D=1 TO 40
40 IF C=1 THEN PRINT CHR$(178); : GOTO 6
0
50 PRINT CHR$(177);
60 C=1-C : NEXT D
70 C=1-C : NEXT K
READY.
```

Let's go through this one line by line, there are a few tricks we've used to draw our wall.

Line 10 – Clear the screen and set the border and background colours.

Line 20 – Set the cursor colour to white and initialise our variable C to equal 1. Keep the variable C in mind, we use this to figure out which character to PRINT.

Line 30 – We set up two FOR … NEXT loops. K goes from 1 to 20 and controls displaying 20 lines of characters. D goes from 1 to 40 and controls displaying 40 columns of characters. Since loop D is nested within loop K, we will basically PRINT the 40 columns of characters (D counts from 1 to 40) on the first line, then when we increment K to 2, we PRINT another 40 columns (again D counts from 1 to 40). This repeats 20 times to PRINT 20 rows of 40 characters each.

Line 40 – We check to see if C is equal to 1. If it is, we PRINT the short T character and then skip down to line 60. If C does not equal 1, we simply drop down one line and execute line 50.

Line 50 – This only executes if C is not equal to 1 (see line 40). It PRINTs out the upside-down short T character.

Line 60 - This first equation is the trick to let us know if we are on an odd or even character. The first time C=1-C runs, C is equal to 1. So line 60 does C=1-1, which sets C to 0. It then loops back to increment D (D+1). The next time this line runs, C will now be equal to 0, so line 60 does C=1-0, which sets C to 1. Each time this runs, C switches between 1 and 0, which causes lines 40 and 50 to PRINT the correct character.

Line 70 – This does the same thing as line 60, but it runs when we need to increment K (loop through the next value of K).

THE TRIANGLE AND RECTANGLE

As you can see in the program above, you don't need to specify each character on the screen individually to produce large shapes or objects. Here are another two programs that use loops to produce large shapes on screen.

```
10  PRINT CHR$(147); CHR$(5)
20  POKE 53280,5 : POKE 53281,0
30  FOR X=1 TO 20
40  FOR N=1 TO 2*X
50  PRINT CHR$(184);
60  NEXT N
70  PRINT
80  NEXT X
```

```
LIST
10 PRINT CHR$(147); CHR$(5)
20 POKE 53280,5 : POKE 53281,0
30 FOR X=1 TO 20
40 FOR N=1 TO 2*X
50 PRINT CHR$(184);
60 NEXT N
70 PRINT
80 NEXT X
READY.
```

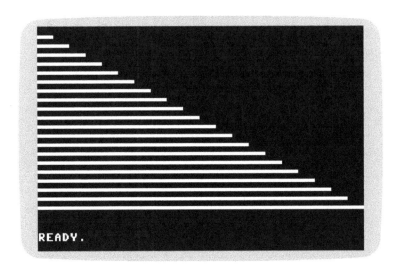

```
10  PRINT CHR$(147); CHR$(31)
20  POKE 53280,0 : POKE 53281,0
30  FOR T=1 TO 18
40  PRINT CHR$(185); : NEXT T
50  PRINT
60  FOR X=1 TO 10
70  PRINT CHR$(165);
80  FOR M=1 TO 16
90  PRINT CHR$(125); : NEXT M
100  PRINT CHR$(167)
110  NEXT X
120  FOR B=1 TO 18
130  PRINT CHR$(184); : NEXT B
```

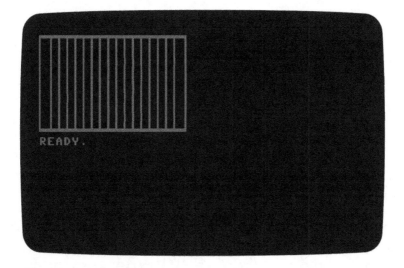

```
LIST

10 PRINT CHR$(147); CHR$(31)
20 POKE 53280,0 : POKE 53281,0
30 FOR T=1 TO 18
40 PRINT CHR$(185); : NEXT T
50 PRINT
60 FOR X=1 TO 10
70 PRINT CHR$(165);
80 FOR M=1 TO 16
90 PRINT CHR$(125); : NEXT M
100 PRINT CHR$(167)
110 NEXT X
120 FOR B=1 TO 18
130 PRINT CHR$(184); : NEXT B
READY.
```

SCREEN MEMORY MAP

Instead of PRINTing characters to the screen using the CHR$
method, you can place any character and colour directly to a specific
position on the screen using the POKE command. Inside the

computer, there are two areas of memory that control the characters displayed on screen. The first area, or map, controls which character is being displayed and the second memory map controls the colour of that character.

If you remember, the Commodore 64 display contains 25 rows with 40 columns each, a total of 1,000 positions on the screen. It makes sense then that the character memory map and the colour memory map are both 1,000 positions long each. The character memory map begins at position 1024 (top left of screen) and continues to position 2023 (bottom right of screen). In the same way, the colour memory map runs from locations 55296 to 56295.

Let's use the colour and memory maps to place a character on screen using POKE.

```
POKE 1024,90 : POKE 55296,1
```

This puts the diamond-shaped character at the top left position on screen and then sets the colour to white.

Instead of having to remember which row and column each memory location refers to, you can use a straightforward mathematical formula to translate the row and column of a position into memory location numbers.

Let's assign Y to represent the row and X to represent the column, but with a special condition that we count the rows and columns starting from 0 (and not from 1). The generic formula for the memory position therefore would be: [first_memory_position]+ (Y*40)+X. Using this we have two commands that will allow you to add any character of any colour anywhere on the screen.

Character
```
POKE 1024+Y*40+X,[character_code]
```
Colour
```
POKE 55296+Y*40+X,[colour_code]
```

Try the following program that will fill your screen with characters one at a time using the screen memory map method.

```
10 POKE 53280,0 : POKE 53281,0
20 FOR X=0 TO 24
30 FOR Y=0 TO 39
40 POKE 1024+Y*40+X,90 : POKE 55296+Y*40+X,1
50 NEXT X
60 NEXT Y
```

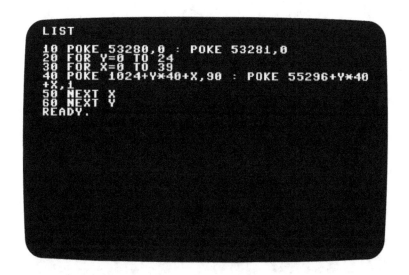

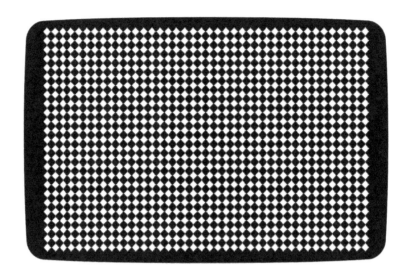

Let's play with the colours a little. Change line 40 to use the value of X as the colour code instead of 1 (white).

```
40 POKE 1024+Y*40+X,90 : POKE 55296+Y*40+X,X
```

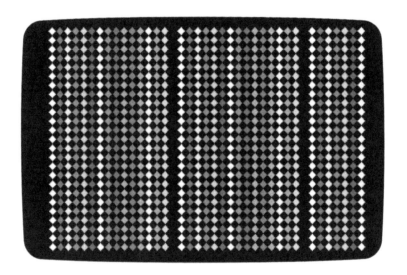

When you run this program now, you will notice that the computer cycles through all 16 colours available to the Commodore 64. Although we only have 16 colours, colour codes 0 to 15, when X climbs high than 15 (it actually goes from 0 to 24), the computer simply cycles through the colour series from the beginning again.

We could change the program a little more to cycle the colours differently again. We can use a variable C to count from 0 to 15 over and over again and use that to specify the colour instead.

Add in these two new lines of code:

```
15 C=0
45 C=C+1 : IF C=16 THEN C=0
```

and change line 40 to use the new colour control variable:

```
40 POKE 1024+Y*40+X,90 : POKE 55296+Y*40+X,X
```

```
LIST
10 POKE 53280,0 : POKE 53281,0
15 C=0
20 FOR Y=0 TO 24
30 FOR X=0 TO 39
40 POKE 1024+Y*40+X,90 : POKE 55296+Y*40
+X,C
45 C=C+1 : IF C=16 THEN C=0
50 NEXT X
60 NEXT Y
70 GOTO 70
READY.
```

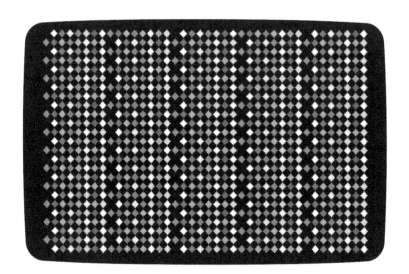

LESSON 9 ANIMATION

Animation on your Commodore 64 in its most basic form involves displaying a character on screen and then moving it in a series of small steps around the screen. As we have learnt in our other lessons, we can use the POKE command to set the position and colour of a character on screen and use loops to programmatically change the position of the character. Let's build a simple animation program together.

```
10 PRINT CHR$(147) : POKE 53280,0 : POKE 53281,0
20 Y=5
30 FOR X=5 TO 20
40 POKE 1024+Y*40+X,86 : POKE 55296+Y*40+X,7
50 NEXT X
```

```
LIST
10 PRINT CHR$(147) : POKE 53280,0 : POKE
   53281,0
20 Y=5
30 FOR X=5 TO 20
40 POKE 1024+Y*40+X,86 : POKE 55296+Y*40
+X,7
50 NEXT X
READY.
```

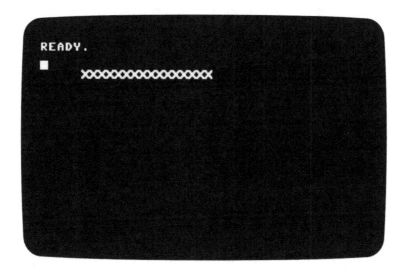

So far, our animation program has highlighted two challenges when attempting animation on the Commodore 64. Firstly, although we have successfully moved the 'X' character from left to right, it still leaves the previously PRINTed character on screen. Secondly, the animation speed is a little too fast. Let's make some improvements.

First, add in a new line to remove the previously displayed character. Since we are only moving in one direction, left to right, we know that the memory position is simply one less than the current position. We can simply change the character to a space (character code 32) at that position.

```
42 POKE 1024+Y*40+X-1,32
```

Now let's add one extra line to slow everything down.

```
44 FOR T=1 TO 50 : NEXT T
```

Run your program again and notice the improvement.

Let's try a different animation program that adds in some extra functionality to do with changing direction. Enter this simple bouncing ball program:

```
10 PRINT CHR$(147) : POKE 53280,0 : POKE 53281,0
20 Y=5 : X=5 : DX=1
30 POKE 1024+Y*40+X,81 : POKE 55296+Y*40+X,5
40 POKE 1024+Y*40+X-DX,32
50 X=X+DX
60 FOR T=1 TO 10 : NEXT T
70 IF X<1 THEN DX=-DX
80 IF X>38 THEN DX=-DX
90 GOTO 30
```

```
LIST
10 PRINT CHR$(147) : POKE 53280,0 : POKE
 53281,0
20 Y=5 : X=5 : DX=1
30 POKE 1024+Y*40+X,81 : POKE 55296+Y*40
+X,5
40 POKE 1024+Y*40+X-DX,32
50 X=X+DX
60 FOR T=1 TO 10 : NEXT T
70 IF X<1 THEN DX=-DX
80 IF X>38 THEN DX=-DX
90 GOTO 30
READY.
```

Line 20 initialises, or sets up, the three variables we will use for this program. X and Y control the coordinates of the character on screen. Y controls the row number and remains the same throughout the program. X controls the column number and changes to move the ball left and right across the screen. DX stands for the Direction of X and controls which way across the screen the ball is currently moving.

Line 30 displays a green ball (character code 81) at the current value of X and Y on the screen. Line 40 clears (or PRINTs a space) at the previous position.

Line 50 moves the ball to the next position for X. If DX is positive, the next position is one more to the right, if it is negative, the position is one to the left.

Lines 70 and 80 are our edge detection checks. If X is less than 1 it means that it has hit the left edge of the screen so we need to switch the direction by changing the sign of DX (in this case DX would equal -1 as the ball is moving left, Line 70 changes DX to equal +1). If X is more than 39, then we have hit the right edge of the screen and need to change the direction again.

This program sets up an infinite loop and your ball will continue bouncing across the screen until you hit the RUN/STOP key.

Let's add some extra colour to our bouncing ball program. Every time we hit a wall (change direction) we want the ball colour to change.

First, we need to set up a variable to hold the value of the colour. Let's use C. Change line 20 to initialise the ball colour to white.

```
20 Y=5 : X=5 : DX=1 : C=1
```

We also need to change Line 30 to use the colour variable.

```
30 POKE 1024+Y*40+X,81 : POKE 55296+Y*40+X,C
```

Next, we need to change the ball colour every time the direction changes, this happens on lines 70 and 80.

```
70 IF X<1 THEN DX=-DX : C=C+1
80 IF X>38 THEN DX=-DX : C=C+1
```

Finally, I like to reset the colour variable once we reach the end of the colour palette (range of colours) for the Commodore 64. So, we need a new line that checks if we have gone past 15 and reset it to 1 (white). (I have skipped the value of 0 because this will display a black ball, and on a black background this will be invisible to us.)

```
85 IF C>15 THEN C=1
```

```
LIST
10 PRINT CHR$(147) : POKE 53280,0 : POKE
   53281,0
20 Y=5 : X=5 : DX=1 : C=1
30 POKE 1024+Y*40+X,81 : POKE 55296+Y*40
+X,C
40 POKE 1024+Y*40+X-DX,32
50 X=X+DX
60 FOR T=1 TO 10 : NEXT T
70 IF X<1 THEN DX=-DX : C=C+1
80 IF X>38 THEN DX=-DX : C=C+1
85 IF C>16 THEN C=1
90 GOTO 30
READY.
```

LESSON 10 DATA BANKS

We have already seen how we can use the INPUT command to get the data we need for our programs from the user when it is running. Another way of using data in your programs is to write them into the code itself. We can store data using the DATA command and fetch this data using the READ command. Try this program that displays the Southern Cross star constellation using the DATA and READ commands.

```
10  PRINT CHR$(147); CHR$(5) : POKE 53280,6 : POKE 53281,6
20  PRINT "SOUTHERN CROSS"
30  DATA 3,18,8,15,17,11,19,8,21,12,21,16,22,9
40  COUNT=7
50  FOR N=1 TO COUNT
60  READ X,Y
70  POKE 1024+Y*40+X,90 : POKE 55296+Y*40+X,1
80  FOR T=1 TO 500 : NEXT T
90  NEXT N
100 GOTO 100
```

```
LIST
10 PRINT CHR$(147); CHR$(5) : POKE 53280
,6 : POKE 53281,6
20 PRINT "SOUTHERN CROSS"
30 DATA 3,18,8,15,17,11,19,8,21,12,21,16
,22,9
40 COUNT=7
50 FOR N=1 TO COUNT
60 READ X,Y
70 POKE 1024+Y*40+X,90 : POKE 55296+Y*40
+X,1
80 FOR T=1 TO 500 : NEXT T
90 NEXT N
100 GOTO 100
READY.
```

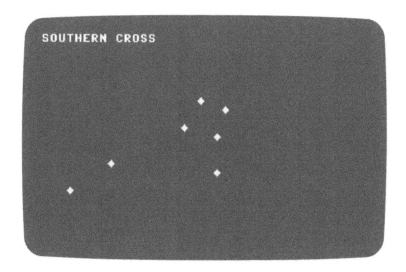

The DATA command on line 30 stores a list of 14 numbers into memory. The READ 60 lets our program know that this list of numbers is understood as pairs of screen coordinates, X and Y. Line 40 sets up the maximum number of times se loop through the DATA set, in this case it lets the computer know that we are expecting 7 pairs of X,Y coordinates.

Using a data bank, we can easily alter just three lines of code (lines 20-40) to display a different constellation. Try changing these three lines for a new constellation.

```
20 PRINT "ORION"
30 DATA 11,6,6,10,15,8,14,16,15,15,16,14,16,22,22,17
40 COUNT=8
```

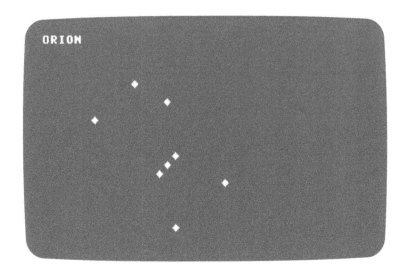

You can also use DATA to store a shape that can be drawn to screen that represents an element of a game. For example, we can build a spaceship out of 2 lines of 4 characters each and store that shape as a list of character codes using the DATA statement.

```
10 PRINT CHR$(147) : POKE 53280,0 : POKE 53281,0
20 DATA 205,105,160,120,68,120,73,119
30 X=10:Y=10
40 FOR N=1 TO 4
50 READ C
60 POKE 1024+Y*40+X,C : POKE 55296+Y*40+X,1
70 READ C
80 POKE 1024+(Y+1)*40+X,C : POKE 55296+(Y+1)*40+X,1
90 X=X+1
100 NEXT N
```

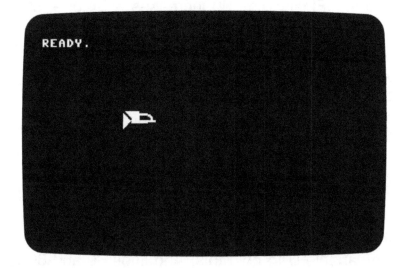

```
LIST
10 PRINT CHR$(147) : POKE 53280,0 : POKE
   53281,0
20 DATA 205,105,160,120,68,120,73,119
30 X=10:Y=10
40 FOR N=1 TO 4
50 READ C
60 POKE 1024+Y*40+X,C : POKE 55296+Y*40+
X,1
70 READ C
80 POKE 1024+(Y+1)*40+X,C : POKE 55296+(
Y+1)*40+X,1
90 X=X+1
100 NEXT N
READY.
```

```
READY.
```

To simplify the loop to draw the spaceship, line 20 actually stores the data by column. That is, the first number is the code for the top left character, the second is for the bottom left, the third is for the top second from left, the third is for the bottom second from the left and so on. This means that we can loop through the columns, writing the top and bottom character as we go from left to right. If we wanted to display each character individually, we would need to nested loops. The outer loop would loop twice, once for the top line and once for the bottom line. The inner loop would need to loop 4 times, once for each character in that line.

Line 30 sets the coordinates of the first character in the star ship in the top left position. You can see that lines 40 and 100 set up the loop that repeats 4 times, once for each column of characters. Lines 50 to 90 repeat 4 times within this loop.

Line 50 reads the top character and line 60 displays it using screen character and colour memory. Similarly, line 70 reads the bottom character and line 80 displays it on screen. You will notice a difference in line 80. It replaces Y*40 with (Y+1)*40. This means that the character will be displayed one row further down, that is, on the second line. Finally, line 90 increases X by one, shifting us to the next column to the right on screen.

Let's extend the use of our data bank to include colour information in addition to character information. So now, instead of single values for each character, we will have pairs of values. The first value controls the character the second will control the colour. Change line 20 to include the new colour values.

```
20 DATA 205,7,105,7,160,7,120,11,68,4,120,11,73,4,119,11
```

We need to change lines 50 and 70 to read this new colour data in, we'll use the variable D to hold this. And lines 60 and 80 to use this colour data.

```
50 READ C,D
60 POKE 1024+Y*40+X,C : POKE 55296+Y*40+X,D
70 READ C,D
80 POKE 1024+(Y+1)*40+X,C : POKE 55296+(Y+1)*40+X,D
```

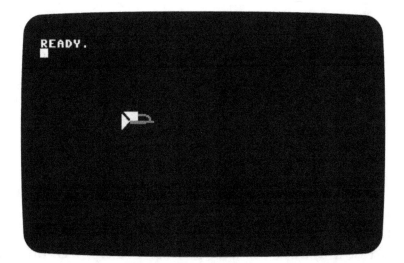

```
LIST

10 PRINT CHR$(147) : POKE 53280,0 : POKE
   53281,0
20 DATA 205,7,105,7,160,7,120,11,68,4,12
   0,11,73,4,119,11
30 X=10:Y=10
40 FOR N=1 TO 4
50 READ C,D
60 POKE 1024+Y*40+X,C : POKE 55296+Y*40+
   X,D
70 READ C,D
80 POKE 1024+(Y+1)*40+X,C : POKE 55296+(
   Y+1)*40+X,D
90 X=X+1
100 NEXT N
READY.
```

```
READY.
```

Now, let's add some code to move our spaceship around the screen in a similar way that we did for our bouncing ball. This time we will move it in both the horizontal and vertical directions.

We need a couple more variables to hold the direction of travel for both X and Y. Change line 30:

```
30 X=10:Y=10:DX=1:DY=-1
```

We need some extra lines to check if we hit the edge of the screen (we give ourselves a bit of a buffer).

```
31 IF X<3 THEN DX=-DX
32 IF X>35 THEN DX=-DX
33 IF Y<2 THEN DY=-DY
34 IF X>19 THEN DY=-DY
```

We add the line that will move the position of our spaceship.

```
35 X=X+DX : Y=Y+DY
```

We have a little issue now that we are using X and Y to move the spaceship around. Our code to draw the spaceship needs a little adjusting to cope with this change. Firstly, line 90 increments X by 1 which helps use draw the next column of characters for our spaceship. This line now interferes with our movement code so let's delete line 90 (simply type in 90 and hit return to delete it).

Now we have an issue where we need to move the code that writes the characters to screen one position to the right every time, we repeat the loop. Luckily, we have a value that increases by 1 with every repeat of the loop, the value N (of course!). Change lines 60 and 80 to use the value for N.

```
60 POKE 1024+Y*40+X+N,C : POKE 55296+Y*40+X+N,D
80 POKE 1024+(Y+1)*40+X+N,C : POKE 55296+(Y+1)*40+X+N,D
```

Finally, we add in a last line that clears the screen and sends the code back up to the start of the code that does the edge check so we can start all over again. We clear the screen as a cheat's way of getting rid of the last position the spaceship was drawn. We should really just erase the 8 previously drawn characters with a space, but to keep this program simple we will do this instead.

```
110 PRINT CHR$(147) : GOTO 31
```

Try run the code.

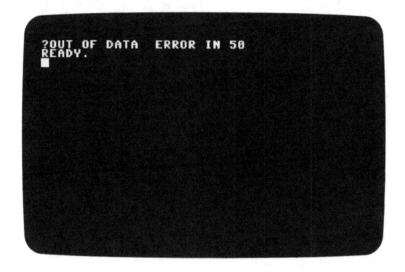

You will see that the space ship is drawn once to the screen, but then the next time it attempts to read the character data using the READ command on line 50 you encounter this ?OUT OF DATA error. This error means that you have asked the computer to read in some more data, but it has already reached the end of the list of data you gave it.

What we really want to happen, is that every time we draw our spaceship, we want to send the computer back to the beginning of our list of data ready to draw it again for the next position. Thankfully there is a command that does exactly that. We will change line 35 to include the new RESTORE command to reset our data list.

```
35 X=X+DX : Y=Y+DY : RESTORE
```

```
LIST
10 PRINT CHR$(147) : POKE 53280,0 : POKE
  53281,0
20 DATA 205,7,105,7,160,7,120,11,68,4,12
0,11,73,4,119,11
30 X=10:Y=10:DX=1:DY=-1
31 IF X<3 THEN DX=-DX
32 IF X>35 THEN DX=-DX
33 IF Y<2 THEN DY=-DY
34 IF Y>19 THEN DY=-DY
35 X=X+DX : Y=Y+DY : RESTORE
40 FOR N=1 TO 4
50 READ C,D
60 POKE 1024+Y*40+X+N,C : POKE 55296+Y*4
0+X+N,D
70 READ C,D
80 POKE 1024+(Y+1)*40+X+N,C : POKE 55296
+(Y+1)*40+X+N,D
100 NEXT N
110 PRINT CHR$(147) : GOTO 31
READY.
```

Run this new version of our code to see the spaceship repeatedly drawn in different positions across the screen. Remember, we have created an infinite loop in line 110 so you need to hit the RUN/STOP key to stop your program running.

LESSON 11 SPRITE GRAPHICS

Using PRINT and POKE to produce text and character-based graphics on screen is not the only way to produce on screen images. Instead of having to constantly draw and erase our graphical objects on screen, we can use Sprites.

A sprite is a two-dimensional image made up of 504 tiny elements called pixels. These pixels are arranged in 21 rows of 24 pixels each. Each sprite is made up of pixels of a single colour and you can have up to 8 sprites on screen at any one time. There is also a multicolour sprite mode available on the Commodore 64. In this mode the pixels become twice as wide, each sprite is now made up of 21 rows of 12 doublewide pixels, but you get up to 4 colours to display your sprite. In this section, we will only look at the single colour, or hi-res sprite mode.

The really useful part of using sprites on the Commodore 64 is that they are controlled using a different area of memory than the screen memory. The shape, position and colour of sprites are controlled by the Video Interface Circuit, or VIC chip. This means we can draw and manipulate our sprites without impacting anything drawn using the screen character and colour memory maps.

DESIGNING A SPRITE

In order to place a sprite into memory, we need to know how the computer understands sprite images. Computers use a different numbering system to us called binary numbers.

In the binary numbering system, there are only 2 digits, 1 or 0. Each digit is referred to as a bit. Everything in the Commodore 64 is arranged into groups of 8 binary digits, or bits and this group of 8 bits is called a byte.

Each position within a byte of data is assigned a particular value, starting from the rightmost bit and moving left. The first bit is assigned the value of 1, the next a value of 2, the next a value of 4 up until the last (or leftmost bit) is assigned a value of 128. The actual value of a bit is equal to 2 to the power of its position number but remember that computers start counting from 0 not 1.

Position Number	7	6	5	4	3	2	1	0
Value	2^7	2^6	2^5	2^4	2^3	2^2	2^1	2^0
Decimal Number	128	64	32	16	8	4	2	1

The value of any particular group of 8 bits (or byte) of data is then calculated by adding up the value of every bit that is set to 1. Let's look at the byte 10001011.

Position Number	7	6	5	4	3	2	1	0
Decimal	128	64	32	16	8	4	2	1
Byte	1	0	0	0	1	0	1	1
Decimal Value	128	0	0	0	8	0	2	1

So, the decimal value of the byte 10001011 is calculated by adding up 128+8+2+1, which equals 139.

Each byte can have a value from 00000000 to 11111111 or 0 to 256. Since we use the decimal value system when we are typing values into the Commodore 64, it is good to know how our decimal numbers relate to the computer's binary-based byte values.

To design your sprites, you first need to put your design into a grid consisting of 24 by 21 pixels. For example, we could re-imagine our character-based spaceship as a sprite.

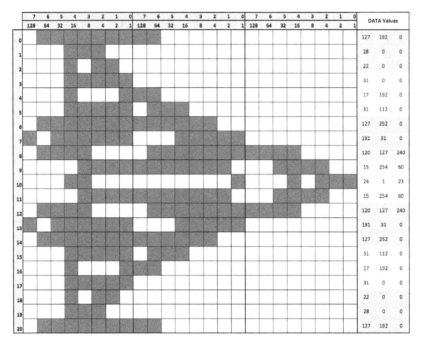

We lay our sprite design into a grid like this so that we can calculate the DATA values we need to enter into the computer to produce it. Remember that your Commodore 64 stores its data in bytes, or groups of 8 bits.

Let's look a bit closer at how we calculate the byte values from our sprite image grid. We take an 8-column portion of our sprite and assign a 1 for every coloured-in pixel and a 0 for every empty pixel. For example, we will calculate the value of the very first byte of sprite data for our spaceship.

128	64	32	16	8	4	2	1	DATA Value
0	1	1	1	1	1	1	1	127

We calculate the value: 64+32+16+8+4+2+1 = 127

Every row in our sprite has 3 groups of 8 pixels. Each group of 8 pixels is used to calculate a byte value, resulting in 3 values for every row. Given that we have 21 rows, we will have a total of 63 bytes. However, because of the way computers are put together 63

97

is an inconvenient number to work with so we add an extra 64th value that is not counted and set it to 0. So, we enter 64 values into our DATA statements for every sprite we want in our programs, the last value always set as 0.

We will take our spaceship sprite, calculate the byte values and enter it into a simple program to display it on screen.

```
10 POKE 53280,4 : POKE 53281,2
20 PRINT CHR$(147)
30 FOR S=0 TO 63
40 READ BYTE
50 POKE 832+S,BYTE
60 NEXT S
70 POKE 2040,13
80 POKE 53287,1
90 POKE 53248,50:POKE 53249,100:POKE 53264,0
100 POKE 53269,1
110 POKE 53271,1:POKE 53277,1
500 DATA 127,192,0,28,0,0,22,0,0
510 DATA 31,0,0,17,192,0,31,112,0
520 DATA 127,252,0,191,31,0,120,127,240
530 DATA 15,254,60,24,1,23,15,254,60
540 DATA 120,127,240,191,31,0,127,252,0
550 DATA 31,112,0,17,192,0,31,0,0
560 DATA 22,0,0,28,0,0,127,192,0,0
```

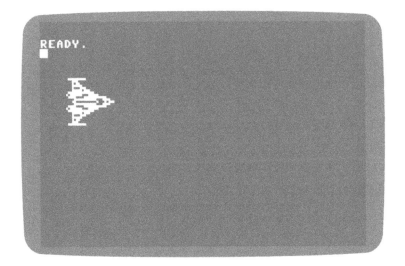

```
LIST
10 POKE 53280,4 : POKE 53281,2
20 PRINT CHR$(147)
30 FOR S=0 TO 63
40 READ BYTE
50 POKE 832+S,BYTE
60 NEXT S
70 POKE 2040,13
80 POKE 53287,1
90 POKE 53248,50:POKE 53249,100:POKE 532
64,0
100 POKE 53269,1
110 POKE 53271,1:POKE 53277,1
500 DATA 127,192,0,28,0,0,22,0,0
510 DATA 31,0,0,17,192,0,31,112,0
520 DATA 127,252,0,191,31,0,120,127,240
530 DATA 15,254,60,24,1,24,15,254,60
540 DATA 120,127,240,191,31,0,127,252,0
550 DATA 31,112,0,17,192,0,31,0,0
560 DATA 22,0,0,28,0,0,127,192,0,0
READY.
```

Looking through the program code, we can see that the data we calculated has been entered into the DATA statements in lines 500 to 560. However, we need to POKE this data into an area of memory that the VIC chip can 'see'. The easiest way to do this is to READ in the sprite data and POKE it into a memory location that the

99

```
540 DATA 120,127,240,191,31,0,127,252,0
550 DATA 31,112,0,17,192,0,31,0,0
560 DATA 22,0,0,28,0,0,127,192,0,0
```

SPRITE COLOURS

You can use any of the Commodore 64's 16 colours for your sprites. It is simply a matter of POKEing the desired colour code into the memory location controlling your sprite's colour. Remember that we can have up to 8 sprites on screen at any one time. We number our sprites from 0 to 7.   For sprite 0, the colour memory location is V+39, for sprite 1 it is V+40 and so on.

Sprite Number	VIC Colour Location	Colour	Code	Colour	Code
0	V+39	Black	0	Orange	8
1	V+40	White	1	Brown	9
2	V+41	Red	2	Light Red	10
3	V+42	Cyan	3	Dark Gray	11
4	V+43	Purple	4	Medium Gray	12
5	V+44	Green	5	Light Green	13
6	V+45	Blue	6	Light Blue	14
7	V+46	Yellow	7	Light Gray	15

SPRITE POSITIONS

To control the position of our sprites we use the sprite location register memory locations. Each sprite has two memory locations to control the X and Y coordinates of the screen. Each of the 8 possible sprites has their own memory location for each of the X and Y positions. These memory locations range from V+0 to V+15 (53248 to 53263). The X and Y coordinates point to the position of the top-left pixel of each sprite.

Sprite Number	X (Horizontal) VIC Location	Y (Vertical) VIC Location
0	V+0	V+1
1	V+2	V+3
2	V+4	V+5
3	V+6	V+7
4	V+8	V+9
5	V+10	V+11
6	V+12	V+13
7	V+14	V+15

There are a possible 256 positions (0-255) for the Y coordinate, which fit perfectly into the byte of data stored in the Y position memory location. However, the screen width has a possible 512 positions (0-511), larger than what can be specified in this one-byte memory location. Earlier we saw that it takes 8 bits of data to store a decimal value up to 255. In order to store up to the value of 511, we need one extra bit, a 9th bit.

Position Number	8	7	6	5	4	3	2	1	0
Decimal Number	256	128	64	32	16	8	4	2	1

A binary number of 111111111 = 1+ 2+ 4+ 8+ 16+ 32+ 64+ 128+ 256 = 511

Instead of giving each sprite's X coordinate an extra byte to store this information we use just one more byte of memory to store this extra bit of information for all our 8 sprites. The term 'most significant bit' refers to the bit that represents the highest value of our X

coordinate, in this case that extra, 9th, bit. What the Commodore 64 VIC chip does is collect all of these extra, most significant bits for the X coordinates for all 8 sprites and stores them together in a single byte in an extra memory location 53264, called the 'X Most Significant Bit' (X-MSB) register. In this value, the first bit belongs to the first sprite, the second bit to the second sprite and so on.

9 bits required to store values 0-511 for X coordinates

```
Sprite 0    01001001
Sprite 1    10001010
Sprite 2    10010001
Sprite 3    01001001
Sprite 4    01010100
Sprite 5    10100010
Sprite 6    01000101
Sprite 7    10000101
```

Take the most significant bit of each 9-bit X coordinate

```
Sprite 0    01001001
Sprite 1    10001010
Sprite 2    10010001
Sprite 3    01001001
Sprite 4    01010100
Sprite 5    10100010
Sprite 6    01000101
Sprite 7    10000101
```

Store these in an additional memory location X-MSB

```
Sprite 0    1001001
Sprite 1    0001010
Sprite 2    0010001
Sprite 3    1001001
Sprite 4    1010100
Sprite 5    0100010
Sprite 6    1000101
Sprite 7    0000101

X-MSB       10100110
```

Let's look at an example. For our first sprite, to which we give the number 0, we store the first 8 bits of the X coordinate in memory location 53248. The 9th bit, the most significant bit, is stored in the first position of the X-MSB at 53264. A value 255 or less only requires the first 8 bits (we always count from right to left) so we set the 9th bit to 0. For example, 139 is represented by the 9-bit number 010001011. We store the first 8 bits (binary 10001011, decimal 139) in location V. That 9th bit, we store in the first position of location V+16, in this case we would store the binary value 00000000 or decimal 0. The BASIC statements would look like this:

```
90 POKE V,139:POKE V+16,0
```

However, for positions larger than 255 we require all 9 bits. For example, the value 264 in binary is 100001000. Again, we store the first 8 bits (binary 00001000, decimal 8) in location V.   That 9th bit, we store in the first position of location V+16, in this case we would store the binary value 00000001 or decimal 1. The BASIC statements would look like this:

```
90 POKE V,8:POKE V+16,1
```

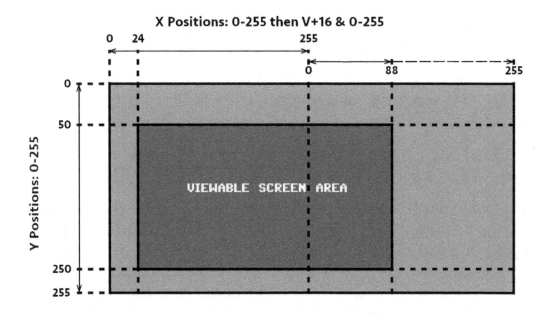

All X positions outside of 24 to 242 and Y positions 50 to 250 are outside of the viewable screen area. This is in order to allow the smooth scrolling of sprites on and off screen in any direction.

Now that you know how to position any of your 8 possible sprites, it is a simple matter of using a loop to move them around the screen.

SPRITE VISIBILITY AND SIZE

Only one bit is needed to turn a single sprite on or off. Again, all the visibility bits for all 8 sprites are collected into a single memory location byte, V+21. For example, if we had multiple sprites defined and we wanted to only turn sprites 0, 2, 4 and 6 on, we would calculate the value to POKE into V+21 as follows:

128	64	32	16	8	4	2	1	Decimal Value
0	1	0	1	0	1	0	1	85

V+21 = 1+4+16+64 = 85

We can also control the vertical and horizontal size of our sprites. Sprites can have their size doubled in either or both directions. Just like we controlled the visibility of all 8 sprites in the single register (V+23), the vertical size is controlled in V+23 and the horizontal size is controlled in V+29.

TOGGLING MULTI-SPRITE REGISTER VALUES

Our multi-sprite registers so far are the X-Most Significant Bit (V+16), Visibility (V+21), Vertical Size (V+23) and Horizontal Size (V+29). Instead of trying to calculate the values of our multi-sprite VIC registers, we can use a little trick to toggle a particular bit on or off, kind of like flicking a switch on or off just for that particular sprite. The really useful thing about this approach is that we don't have to know what the existing value of the VIC register is, we can simply flick the switch for the bit we are interested in and leave the rest alone.

To do this we use 'Bitwise Logical Operators'. The term Bitwise means we are manipulating the number at the level of the individual bits. The term Logical indicates we are using two special mathematical logical operations called AND and OR. Let's look at what each logical operator means when we use it on binary numbers.

For the AND operator, the result will equal 0 unless **both** values equal 1.

```
0 AND 0 = 0
0 AND 1 = 0
1 AND 0 = 0
1 AND 1 = 1
```

For the OR operator, the result will equal to 1 if **either** of the values equal 1.

```
0 OR 0 = 0
0 OR 1 = 1
1 OR 0 = 1
1 OR 1 = 1
```

We can use the AND operator to switch a bit on and the OR operator to switch a bit off.

SWITCH A BIT ON USING OR

Think of the OR operator's action this way. If the value we are using is 0 it leaves the original value alone, if the value is 1 it 'switches' the value to 1.

For example, if we have a couple of sprites already turned on and we want to turn one extra sprite on, we will use bitwise logical manipulation using OR on the V+21 memory register. Say sprites 0 and 3 are already on, and we want to also turn sprite 4 on.

The current value of V+21 would be 9, or 00001001 (bits for sprites 0 and 3 are 'on'). To use the OR operation to turn the bit for sprite 4 'on', we need to use a number that only has bit position 4 on – 00010000. If we perform the OR operation of 00001001 OR 00010000 we get 00011001, effectively switching the bit for sprite 4 on while leaving the rest of the bits alone.

Bit Position	7	6	5	4	3	2	1	0	
Bit Value	128	64	32	16	8	4	2	1	Decimal Value
	0	0	0	0	1	0	0	1	9
OR	0	0	0	1	0	0	0	0	16
	0	0	0	1	1	0	0	1	25

So, the steps to switch sprite 4 ON would be:

1. Fetch (PEEK) the value in V+21
2. OR that with the value of sprite 4's position.
3. Store (POKE) the new value back into V+21

We can do this in Commodore 64 BASIC code that combines these three steps in a single line:

```
POKE V+21,PEEK (V+21) OR 16
```

Using the example above, we can see that we can easily turn any individual bit on by using the OR operation and the value of bit position of the bit you want to turn on.   E.g. Sprite 0 we use the value 1 and for sprite 6 we use the value 64.

SWITCH A BIT OFF USING AND

Think of the AND operator's action this way. If the value we are using is 1 it leaves the original value alone, if the value is 0 it 'switches' the value to 0. For example, we now want to turn sprite 4 back off while leaving the other two sprites alone.

The current value of V+21 would be 25, or 00011001 (bits for sprites 0, 3 and 4 are 'on'). To use the AND operation to turn the bit for sprite 4 'on', we need to use a number that only has bit position 4 off – 11101111. If we perform the AND operation of 00011001 OR 11101111 we get 00001001, effectively switching the bit for sprite 4 off while leaving the rest of the bits alone.

Bit Position	7	6	5	4	3	2	1	0	
Bit Value	128	64	32	16	8	4	2	1	Decimal Value
	0	0	0	1	1	0	0	1	25
AND	1	1	1	0	1	1	1	1	239
	0	0	0	0	1	0	0	1	9

So, the steps to switch sprite 4 OFF would be:

1. Fetch (PEEK) the value in V+21
2. ABD that with the value of sprite 4's position off.
3. Store (POKE) the new value back into V+21

We can do this in Commodore 64 BASIC code that combines these three steps in a single line:

```
POKE V+21,PEEK (V+21) AND 239
```

Using the example above, we can see that we can easily turn any individual bit off by using the AND operation and the value of bit position of the bit you want to turn off. You can easily calculate this number by subtracting the value of the bit position from 255. For example, for sprite 4 we calculate 255-16=239, for sprite 6 we do 255-64=191.

TWO SPRITES AND ANIMATION

Let's create a short program that animates two separate sprites on the screen at once. We'll use our original spaceship sprite and a new tank sprite.

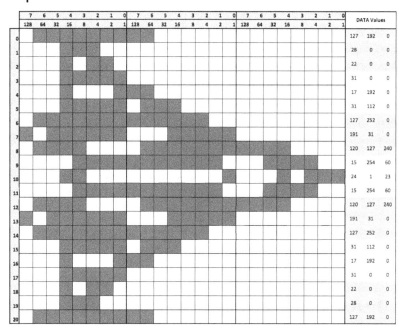

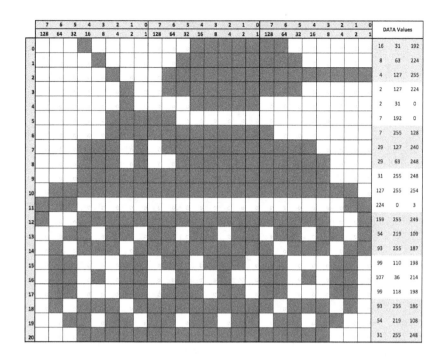

	DATA Values		
0	16	31	192
1	8	63	224
2	4	127	255
3	2	127	224
4	2	31	0
5	7	192	0
6	7	255	128
7	29	127	240
8	29	63	248
9	31	255	248
10	127	255	254
11	224	0	3
12	159	255	249
13	54	219	109
14	93	255	187
15	99	110	198
16	107	36	214
17	99	118	198
18	93	255	186
19	54	219	108
20	31	255	248

```
10  PRINT CHR$(147);CHR$(19);
20  POKE 53280,2:POKE 53281,5
30  PRINT CHR$(18);CHR$(154);
40  V=53248:FOR S=1 TO 15
50  PRINT "                                  ";:NEXT S
60  FOR C=0 TO 127:READ BYTE
70  POKE 832+C,BYTE:NEXT C
80  X0=80:Y0=75:X1=0:Y1=190
90  D0=4:D1=1
100 POKE 2040,13:POKE 2041,14
110 POKE V+39,7:POKE V+40,0
120 POKE V+21,3
130 T0=INT(X0/256):T1=INT(X1/256)
140 POKE V+16,T0+2*T1
150 POKE V,X0-T0*256:POKE V+1,Y0
160 POKE V+2,X1-T1*256:POKE V+4,Y1
```

```
170 IF X0>300 THEN D0=-D0
180 IF X0<50 THEN D0=-D0
190 IF X1>350 THEN X1=0
200 X0=X0+D0:X1=X1+D1:GOTO 130
500 DATA 127,192,0,28,0,0,22,0,0
510 DATA 31,0,0,17,192,0,31,112,0
520 DATA 127,252,0,191,31,0,120,127,240
530 DATA 15,254,60,24,1,23,15,254,60
540 DATA 120,127,240,191,31,0,127,252,0
550 DATA 31,112,0,17,192,0,31,0,0
560 DATA 22,0,0,28,0,0,127,192,0,0
570 DATA 16,31,192,8,63,224,4,127,255
580 DATA 2,127,224,2,31,0,7,192,0
590 DATA 7,255,128,29,127,240,29,63,248
600 DATA 31,255,248,127,255,254,224,0,3
610 DATA 159,255,249,54,219,109,93,255,187
620 DATA 99,110,198,107,36,214,99,118,198
630 DATA 93,255,186,54,219,108,31,255,248,0
```

```
10 PRINT CHR$(147);CHR$(19);
20 POKE 53280,2:POKE 53281,5
30 PRINT CHR$(18);CHR$(154);
40 V=53248:FOR S=1 TO 15
50 PRINT "          ";:NEXT S
60 FOR C=0 TO 127:READ BYTE
70 POKE 832+C,BYTE:NEXT C
80 X0=80:Y0=75:X1=0:Y1=190
90 D0=4:D1=1
100 POKE 2040,13:POKE 2041,14
110 POKE V+39,7:POKE V+40,0
120 POKE V+21,3
130 T0=INT(X0/256):T1=INT(X1/256)
140 POKE V+16,T0+2*T1
150 POKE V,X0-T0*256:POKE V+1,Y0
160 POKE V+2,X1-T1*256:POKE V+3,Y1
170 IF X0>300 THEN D0=-D0
180 IF X0<50 THEN D0=-D0
190 IF X1>350 THEN X1=0
200 X0=X0+D0:X1=X1+D1:GOTO 130

READY.
■
```

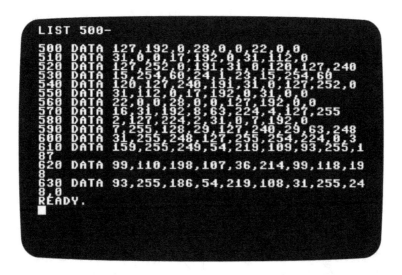

```
LIST 500-
500 DATA 127,192,0,28,0,0,22,0,0
510 DATA 31,0,0,17,192,0,31,112,0
520 DATA 127,252,0,191,31,0,120,127,240
530 DATA 15,254,60,24,1,23,15,254,60
540 DATA 120,127,240,191,31,0,127,252,0
550 DATA 31,112,0,17,192,0,31,0,0
560 DATA 22,0,0,28,0,0,127,192,0,0
570 DATA 16,31,192,8,63,224,4,127,255
580 DATA 2,127,224,2,31,0,7,192,0
590 DATA 7,255,128,29,127,240,29,63,248
600 DATA 31,255,248,127,255,254,224,0,3
610 DATA 159,255,249,54,219,109,93,255,1
87
620 DATA 99,110,198,107,36,214,99,118,19
8
630 DATA 93,255,186,54,219,108,31,255,24
8,0
READY.
```

Lines 500 to 630 are our DATA statements for both our sprites.

Lines 10 to 50 set up the colours and the background. Can you see the two-colour background effect is made by setting the screen background to light green and then PRINTing 15 lines of light blue spaces (40 per line) at the top of the screen?

Lines 60 and 70 store the sprite data into our memory locations.

Lines 80 and 90 set up our initial X and Y coordinates and direction and speed for both our sprites. Notice how setting D0 to 4 will mean that our sprite 0 will travel 4 times faster than sprite 1?

Line 100 sets the start memory location of both our sprites. Line 110 sets the colours of the sprites and then line 120 sets both our sprites visibility to on.

Line 130 has a little trick to calculate if we need to set the extra bit in the X-Most Significant Bit (X-MSB) register. Remember, this bit only needs to be set if the value of the X coordinate is larger than 256. This line will set T0 and T1 to 1 only if the value of the matching X coordinate is larger than 256. Line 140 will set the appropriate value for the X-MSB register using the T0 and T1 values. Then lines 150 and 160 will set the X and Y values or our two sprites, taking into account if the X value is larger than 255.

Lines 170 to 190 perform our screen boundary checks for our sprites. For sprite 0, which uses X0, if the sprite approaches the edge of the screen, we simply reverse the direction of travel. For sprite 1 we reset the value of X1 to 0 once it passes off the right edge of the screen, effectively continually scrolling the tank from left to right.

Finally, line 200 increments the X position values of both sprites and loops back to the top of the code that performs the sprite movements.

LESSON 12 SOUNDS AND SPECIAL EFFECTS

Sounds on the Commodore 64 are created within the Sound Interface Device, or SID chip. All your sounds, sound effects and music are controlled using the 29 memory locations starting at 54272. In much the same way we use V+Offset to refer to the VIC chip memory locations, we use the S+Offset method to refer to the SID chip locations. The SID chip can control 3 independent sound-making channels or voices. The memory addresses for controlling sound are below (we won't worry about S+25-28 because they are read-only values that we will not use).

Function	Channel / Voice		
	1	2	3
Note Frequency (Low Value)	S+0	S+7	S+14
Note Frequency (High Value)	S+1	S+8	S+15
Pulse Width (Low Value)	S+2	S+9	S+16
Pulse Width (Low Value)	S+3	S+10	S+17
Waveform and Channel Control	S+4	S+11	S+18
Envelope (Attack/Delay)	S+5	S+12	S+19
Envelope (Sustain/Release)	S+6	S+13	S+20
Filter Cut-off (Low Value)		S+21	
Filter Cut-off (High Value)		S+22	
Filter Control		S+23	
Filter Mode / Main Volume		S+24	

FIRST SOUND PROGRAM

Try this first little program to make your first sound on the Commodore 64.

```
10 S=54272:POKE S+24,15
20 POKE S+5,0:POKE S+6,240
30 POKE S+4,33
40 POKE S,0:POKE S+1,40
50 FOR T=1 TO 1000:NEXT T
60 POKE S+4,32
```

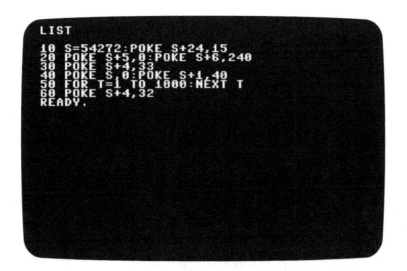

Line 10 sets the start value of the SID chip memory locations, S. It then sets the master volume, S+24 to 15. The volume of the SID chip can be set from 0 (off) to 15 (maximum).

THE ADSR ENVELOPE

Line 20 sets up what is called the 'sound envelope' shape. Sounds in the real world rarely just start and stop suddenly. They tend to grow in volume, stay at that volume for some time and then fade away. We simulate this using the attack, decay, sustain, release (ADSR) approach to sound synthesisers.

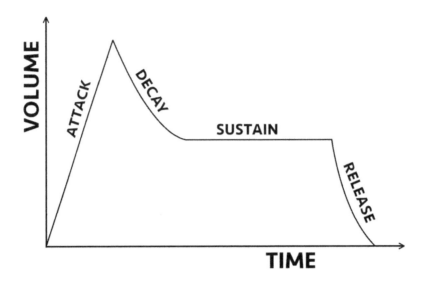

Attack is the rate at which the sound first rises from zero to its peak volume. Then the sound falls off slightly to some middle-range volume. The rate of this fall from the peak volume to the middle-range volume is called the **Decay**. That middle-range volume itself is called the **Sustain**. And finally, once the sound has stopped playing, it falls from the Sustain volume back down to zero. The rate of that final drop is called the **Release**.

Each of the ADSR values can range from 0 to 15. The sustain setting is simply a volume level from 0 (off) to 15 (maximum). The attack, decay and release settings are translated into times according to the following table of values.

Value	Attack	Decay	Release
0	2 ms	6 ms	6 ms
1	8 ms	24 ms	24 ms
2	16 ms	48 ms	48 ms
3	24 ms	72 ms	72 ms
4	38 ms	114 ms	114 ms
5	56 ms	168 ms	168 ms
6	68 ms	204 ms	204 ms
7	80 ms	240 ms	240 ms
8	100 ms	0.3 s	0.3 s
9	0.25 s	0.75 s	0.75 s
10	0.5 s	1.5 s	1.5 s
11	0.8 s	2.4 s	2.4 s
12	1 s	3 s	3 s
13	3 s	9 s	9 s
14	5 s	15 s	15 s
15	8 s	24 s	24 s

Using binary numbering, we only need 4 bits (called a nibble, a nibble is half a byte) to store a number up to 15. Since we only need 4 bits each, the Commodore 64 combines the attack and delay values into one memory register and the sustain and release values into the other.

Let's look at how we could combine the attack/decay vale for voice 1 in S+5. We want to set the attack rate to 1 second (a decimal value of 12, binary 1100) and the decay rate to 204 milliseconds (a decimal value of 6, binary 0110).

Separately, these values look like this.

8	4	2	1	Attack	8	4	2	1	Decay
1	1	0	0	12	0	1	1	0	6

However, you need to combine them into a single byte value so we can POKE that value into the S+5 memory register.

128	64	32	16	8	4	2	1	Decimal Value
1	1	0	0	0	1	1	0	198

The BASIC statement to store this part of the ADSR envelope would be:

```
POKE S+5,198
```

Similarly, let's set the sustain value to 11 and release to 1.5 seconds (decimal value 10).

8	4	2	1	Sustain	8	4	2	1	Release
1	0	1	1	11	1	0	1	0	10

128	64	32	16	8	4	2	1	Decimal Value
1	0	1	1	1	0	1	0	186

The BASIC statement to store this part of the ADSR envelope would be:

```
POKE S+6,186
```

In our current sound playing code, our ADSR envelope is set up with the attack/decay value of 0 (binary 00000000) and the sustain/release value of 240 (11110000). Splitting these up into their separate nibble values we can see that the attack and decay values are 0 (instantaneous), the sustain volume is 15 (full volume) and the release value is 0 (also instantaneous).

The ADSR envelope will look something like this:

To change our ADSR envelope to use the values we explored above – attack=1 sec, decays=204 ms, sustain=11 and release=1.5 sec – we need to change line 20 to:

```
20 POKE S+5,198:POKE S+6,186
```

This will have an ADSR envelope that will look something like this instead:

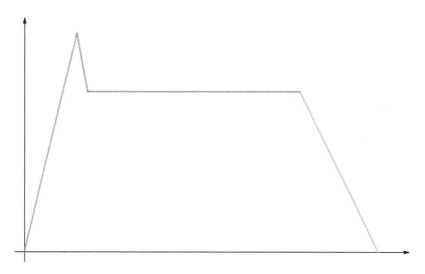

Can you notice the change in the sound played?

SOUND WAVEFORMS

Different sounds can be created by specifying the kind of waveform that is used to generate that sound. The Commodore 64 can generate four different types of waveforms.

Triangle

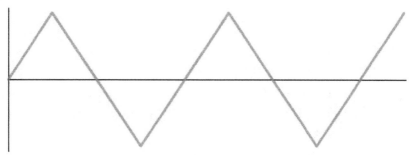

Sawtooth

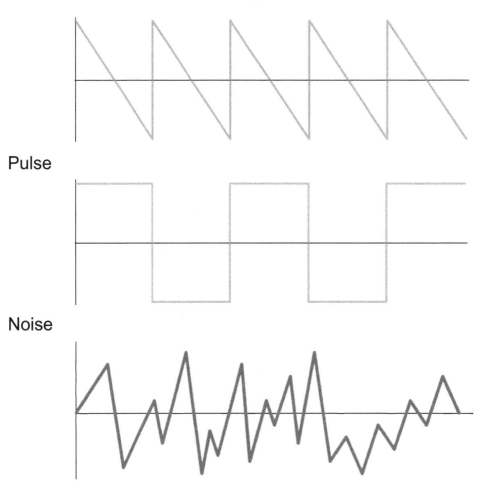

Pulse

Noise

You set the waveform using the waveform and channel control memory register, which for voice 1 is S+4. Like our ADSR envelope registers, the waveform and channel control register has separated the value of the byte into several parts, which each bit set representing various settings.

7	6	5	4	3	2	1	0
Noise	Pulse	Sawtooth	Triangle	Test	Ring Modulation	Syncronise	Gate

At this stage, we will only use bits 0, 4, 5, 6, and 7. Bit 0 is called the 'gate' and controls whether the voice or channel is currently playing a sound or not. Think of it like it is a key on a piano keyboard. If you press the key down the gate is set to 1 and a sound plays. When you release the key, the gate is set to 0 and the sound stops.

Bits 4 to 7 control which waveform you want the voice to use. You only set one of these bits at any one time. For example, to set the triangle waveform you use the value 16. However, to actually play a sound the gate needs to be 'on', making the value 17. When you want the sound to stop, turn the gate 'off' by setting the value to 16. The rule is then, that to play a sound, simply add 1 to the value of the waveform you want to use.

Waveform	Sound On	Sound Off
Triangle	17	16
Sawtooth	33	32
Pulse	65	64
Noise	129	128

Change the waveform being used in our sound program by changing lines 30 (sound on) and 60 (sound off). Currently we are using the sawtooth waveform. Experiment with the other waveforms and see how they sound. For example, change it to the triangle waveform.

```
30 POKE S+4,17
60 POKE S+4,16
```

If you tried using the pulse waveform, you would not have heard anything. This is because for this waveform we need to specify an additional setting, the pulse width. The pulse width setting is actually 12 bits long.   This means that the setting is split between two memory registers, the first holds the low byte – the 8 least significant bits and the second holds the high nibble value – the remaining 4 most significant bits.

2048	1024	512	256	128	64	32	16	8	4	2	1
0	0	0	0	0	0	0	0	0	0	0	0

	128	64	32	16	8	4	2	1
POKE S+2	0	0	0	0	0	0	0	0
	x	x	x	x	8	4	2	1
POKE S+3	-	-	-	-	0	0	0	0

The higher the value for the pulse width, the greater the percentage of the pulse cycle will be set high.   The actual formula for working out this percentage is PW High = (PW Setting/40.95)%

So, to get a square wave, one that is evenly high and low, you need to set the pulse width to 2048. Since the setting is split over the two registers you would set the low value to 0 and the high value to 8.

Don't worry about trying to figure this all out right away.   Instead keep it simple by always setting the low value to 0 and the high value to one of the following values.

Pulse Width	Low Value	High Value
25%	0	4
50%	0	8
75%	0	12

For example, to set the pulse width to 50% for voice 1 you would use the following BASIC statement in your code:

```
POKE S+2,0:POKE S+3,8
```

To use a pulse waveform in our sample code, change the lines 30 and 60 to use the pulse waveform value and add a new line 35 to specify the pulse width.

Your code should now look like this:

```
10 S=54272:POKE S+24,15
20 POKE S+5,0:POKE S+6,240
30 POKE S+4,65
35 POKE S+2,0:POKE S+3,8
40 POKE S,0:POKE S+1,40
50 FOR T=1 TO 1000:NEXT T
60 POKE S+4,64
```

```
LIST
10 S=54272:POKE S+24,15
20 POKE S+5,198:POKE S+6,186
30 POKE S+4,65
35 POKE S+2,0   :POKE S+3,8
40 POKE S,0:POKE S+1,40
50 FOR T=1 TO 1000:NEXT T
60 POKE S+4,64
READY.
```

NOTES AND FREQUENCY

The frequency describes the pitch of the sound, how high or low the note is being played. The value of the frequency uses a 16-bit value. Since we can only store 8 bits per memory register, the frequency value is split into two 8-bit values, the 8 least significant bits are stored in the low value register and the 8 most significant bits are stored in the high value register. For voice 1 these are S+0 and S+1.

You can calculate the frequency setting you need to enter using the formula below.

Note Frequency * 256^3 / Clock Speed

Where the clock speed for the original Commodore 64 was:
PAL: 985248

NTSC: 1022727

So, for a middle C (C-4) note at 261.63Hz running on a PAL system you would calculate:

261.63 * 256^3 / 985248 = 4455

Then to calculate the high and low frequency values for the SID chip:

1. Divide the frequency result by 256

2. The quotient of the result (the whole number before the decimal point) is your high value number.

3. Multiply the remainder (the number after the decimal point) by 256 to get your low value number.

So, for our middle C note we do the following:

1. 4455/256 = 17.4023438

2. 17 is our high setting value

3. 0.4023438 x 256 = 103 - this is our low setting value

For voice 1 we would then use the following code to program in a middle C note.

```
POKE S+0,103 : POKE S+1,17
```

Instead of calculating all our notes manually, we can use frequency value tables to look up the values instead.

Octave	PAL Frequency values: high, low. Voice 1: POKE S+0, [low] : POKE S+1,[high]											
7	139 57	147 128	156 69	165 144	175 104	185 214	196 227	208 153	221 0	234 36	248 16	
6	69 156	73 192	78 35	82 200	87 180	92 235	98 114	104 76	110 128	117 18	124 8	131 104
5	34 206	36 224	39 17	41 100	43 218	46 118	49 57	52 38	55 64	58 137	62 4	65 180
4	17 103	18 112	19 137	20 178	21 237	23 59	24 156	26 19	27 160	29 69	31 2	32 218
3	8 180	9 56	9 196	10 89	10 247	11 157	12 78	13 10	13 208	14 162	15 129	16 109
2	4 90	4 156	4 226	5 45	5 123	5 207	6 39	6 133	6 232	7 81	7 193	8 55
1	2 45	2 78	2 113	2 150	2 190	2 231	3 20	3 66	3 116	3 169	3 224	4 27
0	1 22	1 39	1 57	1 75	1 95	1 116	1 138	1 161	1 186	1 212	1 240	2 14
Note	C	C# Db	D	D# Eb	E	F	F# Gb	G	G# Ab	A	A# Bb	B

SOUND EFFECTS

Using the noise waveform, you can program a range of sound effects.

GUNFIRE

```
10 S=54272:POKE S+24,15
20 POKE S+5,6:POKE 2+6,89
30 POKE S+0,0:POKE S+1,50
40 FOR K=1 TO 10
50 POKE S+4,129
60 FOR T=1 TO 65:NEXT T
70 POKE S+4,128
80 NEXT K
```

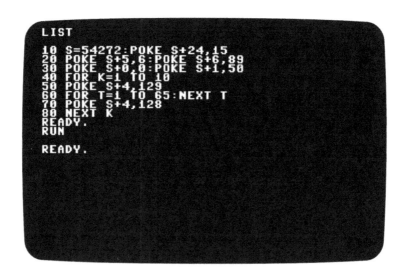

```
LIST
10 S=54272:POKE S+24,15
20 POKE S+5,6:POKE S+6,89
30 POKE S+0,0:POKE S+1,50
40 FOR K=1 TO 10
50 POKE S+4,129
60 FOR T=1 TO 65:NEXT T
70 POKE S+4,128
80 NEXT K
READY.
RUN

READY.
```

This code produces the sound of a short machine gun blast. Line 20 sets up the ADSR envelope to quickly rise to its maximum volume, decays fast to about half volume before dying away fairly slowly.

LASER GUN

```
10 S=54272:POKE S+24,15
```

131

```
20 POKE S+5,0:POKE S+6,249
30 POKE S+0,0:POKE S+4,129
40 FOR C=0 TO 8
50 POKE S+1,44-C*4
60 FOR T=1 TO 30:NET T
70 NEXT C
80 POKE S+4,128
```

```
LIST
10 S=54272:POKE S+24,15
20 POKE S+5,0:POKE S+6,249
30 POKE S+0,0:POKE S+4,129
40 FOR C=0 TO 8
50 POKE S+1,44-C*4
60 FOR T=1 TO 30:NEXT T
70 NEXT C
80 POKE S+4,128
READY.
```

The laser gun sound demonstrates the impact of rapidly changing
the frequency while playing the sound. Lines 40 to 70 rapidly
change the frequency using a FOR … NEXT loop.

BIRD CHIRPING

```
10 S=54272:POKE S+24,15
20 POKE S+5,0:POKE S+6,249
30 K=1
40 POKE S+0,0:POKE S+1,100
50 POKE S+3,8:POKE S+4,65
```

```
60 FOR T=1 TO 60:NEXT T
70 POKE S+4,65:FOR C=0 TO 6
80 POKE S+1,C*15+150
90 NEXT C:POKE S+4,0
100 FOR T=1 TO 200:NEXT T
110 K=K+1:IF K=2 THEN 70
120 FOR T=1 TO 250:NEXT T: GOTO 30
```

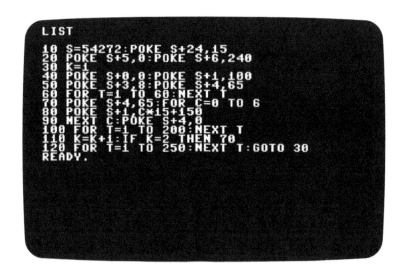

You will need to hit the RUN/STOP key once you have finished listening to the bird chirp sound effect.

The bird chirp sound effect uses the pulse waveform and like the laser gun effect, uses a FOR … NEXT loop to rapidly change the frequency of the sound. In this case, we play two kinds of sounds to produce our effect. A low sound is played in lines 40 to 50 and the rapidly changing high sound is looped twice in lines 70 to 110. Line 120 loops back to the start of sound making part of the code to continue indefinitely.

MUSIC AND CHORDS

So far, we have experimented with sound effects and simple notes.
We can use a short program that reads in DATA to play a tune.

```
10 S=54272:POKE S+24,15
20 POKE S+5,0:POKE S+6,160
30 READ H,L,D
40 IF H<0 THEN END
50 IF H=0 THEN POKE S+4,32:GOTO 80
60 POKE S+0,L:POKE S+1,H
70 POKE S+4,33
80 FOR T=1 TO D*100:NEXT T
90 POKE S+4,32
100 GOTO 30
110 DATA 0,0,2,52,8,1,43,218,1,52,8,2
120 DATA 49,57,2,41,100,2,43,218,2,39,17,1
130 DATA 39,17,1,39,17,2,36,224,1,36,224,1
140 DATA 36,224,2,34,206,1,34,206,1,34,206,2
150 DATA 32,218,1,43,218,1,34,206,1,43,218,1
160 DATA 32,218,2,0,0,2,-1,0,0
```

```
LIST
10 S=54272:POKE 2+24,15
20 POKE S+5,0:POKE S+6,160
30 READ H,L,D
40 IF H<0 THEN END
50 IF H=0 THEN POKE S+4,32:GOTO 80
60 POKE S+0,L:POKE S+1,H
70 POKE S+4,33
80 FOR T=1 TO D*100:NEXT T
90 POKE S+4,32
100 GOTO 30
110 DATA 0,0,2,52,8,1,43,218,1,52,8,2
120 DATA 49,57,2,41,100,2,43,218,2,39,17
1
130 DATA 39,17,1,39,17,2,36,224,1,36,224
1
140 DATA 36,224,2,34,206,1,34,206,1,34,2
06,2
150 DATA 32,218,1,43,218,1,34,206,1,43,2
18,1
160 DATA 32,218,2,0,0,2,-1,0,0
READY.
```

The tune is 4 bars from the tune Dance of the Sugar Plum Fairy by Tchaikovsky.

We have used DATA statements to store in 3 numbers for each note, the frequency high value, the frequency low value and the duration. Line 30 reads each of these numbers into H, L and D respectively.

To stop the tune playing, we enter a negative number in for the H value. Line 40 checks for this and ends the program if it finds it. Notice our last three numbers in the DATA statements in line 160 are -1,0,0. We still have to place three numbers so that our READ statement works, but the last two numbers can be anything because we don't use them. I've used zeros as it is easier to recognise when you are reading through the code.

If we want to play nothing, or silence, for a portion of the tune, we set H to 0 (zero) and set the duration we want the silence to last for. Line 50 checks for this and sets voice 1's gate bit to off (and so stopping any sound playing) and then sips down to line 80 where the duration is handled.

Now, if H is greater than 1, this means we want to actually play a note. Lines 60 and 70 handle the frequency setting and start the note playing.

Line 80 handles the duration we specify in the third of our numbers. In this program we assume that the shortest note we will play is a quarter note and assign the value of the duration for these notes as 1. We then use a duration of 2 for half notes and 4 for full notes. Then line 80 multiplies the duration value by a length that will correspond to how long we want a quarter note to play for. Larger values will slow down the tune and smaller values will speed up the tempo.

Once the note has finished playing, we stop the sound (close the gate bit) on voice 1 and loop back to the start of our tune-handling code.

The DATA statements values were derived by taking the sheet music for these 4 bars and using the PAL note frequency table to look up the high and low value settings for each.

CHORDS

So far, we have only used voice 1 to play a single note at a time. However, there are three voices that can all play a different sound or note at the same time. This means we can play music that involves chords of up to three notes at any one time. Let's enhance our tune above to use two voices, adding an extra one for the base clef.

```
10 S=54272:POKE S+24,15
20 POKE S+5,0:POKE S+6,160
30 POKE S+12,0:POKE S+13,160
40 READ C
50 IF C=-5 THEN GOTO 130
60 IF C=-1 THEN FOR T=1 TO 100:NEXT T:GOTO 40
70 READ H,L
80 POKE S+(C*7)-3,32
90 IF H=0 THEN GOTO 40
100 POKE S+(C*7)-7,L:POKE S+(C*7)-6,H
110 POKE S+(C*7)-3,33
120 GOTO 40
130 POKE S+4,32:POKE S+11,32:END
200 DATA 1,0,0,2,10,247,-1,-1
210 DATA 1,52,38,2,13,10,-1,1,43,218,-1
220 DATA 1,52,38,2,10,247,-1,-1
230 DATA 1,49,57,2,14,162,-1,-1
240 DATA 1,41,100,2,10,247,-1,-1
250 DATA 1,43,218,2,15,129,-1,-1
```

```
260 DATA 1,39,17,2,10,247,-1,1,39,17,-1
270 DATA 1,39,17,2,16,109,-1,-1
280 DATA 1,36,224,2,10,247,-1,1,36,224,-1
290 DATA 1,36,224,2,18,112,-1,-1
300 DATA 1,34,206,2,10,247,-1,1,34,206,-1
310 DATA 1,34,206,2,19,137,-1,-1
320 DATA 1,32,218,2,10,247,-1,1,43,218,-1
330 DATA 1,34,206,2,10,247,-1,1,43,218,-1
340 DATA 1,32,218,2,10,247,-1,-1
350 DATA 1,0,0,2,0,0,-1,-1
500 DATA -5
```

```
LIST -130

10 S=54272:POKE 2+24,15
20 POKE S+5,0:POKE S+6,160
30 POKE S+12,0:POKE S+13,160
40 READ C
50 IF C=-5 THEN GOTO 130
60 IF C=-1 THEN FOR T=1 TO 100:NEXT T:GO
TO 40
70 READ H,L
80 POKE S+(C*7)-3,32
90 IF H=0 THEN GOTO 40
100 POKE S+(C*7)-7,L:POKE S+(C*7)-6,H
110 POKE S+(C*7)-3,33
120 GOTO 40
130 POKE S+4,32:POKE S+11,32:END

READY.
■
```

```
LIST 200-

200 DATA 1,0,0,2,10,247,-1,-1
210 DATA 1,52,38,2,13,10,-1,1,43,218,-1
220 DATA 1,52,38,2,10,247,-1,-1
230 DATA 1,49,57,2,14,162,-1,-1
240 DATA 1,41,100,2,10,247,-1,-1
250 DATA 1,43,218,2,15,129,-1,-1
260 DATA 1,39,17,2,10,247,-1,1,39,17,-1
270 DATA 1,39,17,2,16,109,-1,-1
280 DATA 1,36,224,2,10,247,-1,1,36,224,-
1
290 DATA 1,36,224,2,18,112,-1,-1
300 DATA 1,34,206,2,10,247,-1,1,34,206,-
1
310 DATA 1,34,206,2,19,137,-1,-1
320 DATA 1,32,218,2,10,247,-1,1,43,218,-
1
330 DATA 1,32,218,2,10,247,-1,1,43,218,-
1
340 DATA 1,32,218,2,10,247,-1,-1
350 DATA 1,0,0,2,0,0,-1,-1
500 DATA -5
READY.
```

Lines 10 to 30 set up the SID chip volume and ADSR envelopes for both voices 1 and 2.

In this program, we don't need to specify the duration in our DATA statements. Instead, we just specify which notes, or silence, that is playing on each voice for every half-note duration of time. We specify the high and low value frequency for each note just like before, but this time we have to specify the voice number as well as another special control value.

Look at the DATA in line 220. The first 3 numbers (1,52,38) tell the code to play the note G-5 on voice 1 and the next 3 (2,10,247) play E-3 on voice 2. So, our DATA generally follows the pattern Voice, High, Low values. Like our previous program, if we set the High value to 0 (zero) we want that voice to be silent (e.g. 1,0,0 sets voice 1 to silent).

In this program, when our tune is complete, we simply pass a -5 as the voice number. Line 50 detects this and sends us to line 130 where we silence both our voices and ends the program.

Instead of specifying the note and duration, we have 'sliced' our tune into quarter-note durations and only specify what each voice is playing during each quarter-note slice of time. This program makes use of the fact that once you set a sound playing on the SID chip, it will keep on playing it until you turn off that voice or specify a different sound to play. So, if a not plays longer than a quarter not duration, we don't do anything and just let it keep on playing. The basic approach is that we set the note playing on voice 1, then the note playing on voice 2 and then send the code a value of -1 to let it know to move on to the next quarter-note slice of time. The steps our code uses to play our tune using the DATA statements looks like this:

1. Get the next value from the DATA statement.

Line 40 reads the value into the variable C.

2. If C equals -5, we stop all sounds and end the program, see line 50.

3. If C equals -1, this means we have reached the end the data for this quarter-note slice of time. Line 60 pauses the code for the note duration to let everything play and then start back at step 1.

4. If C is equal to 1 or 2, it means we want to specify something to play on voice 1 or 2.

5. We then fetch 2 more values, H and L for the high and low value frequency setting, line 70.

6. Turn off the sound for this voice in line 80. This means that we can either play a new note or silence.

We select the correct S+Index value by using a trick with the voice number (C).

7. If H equals 0, we want silence on this voice, so line 90 leaves the sound off for this voice and we go back to step 1.

8. Otherwise, set the high and low values and turn the sound on for this voice. Lines 100 to 120 process this and then sends us back to step 1.

Look at the DATA inline 210. The first 3 numbers specify the note for voice 1, the second 3 numbers set the note for voice 2. Then we pass a -1 value to tell our code to play this for a quarter-note duration. The next 3 numbers change the note for voice 1 and then we send another -1 value to tell the code to play this for the next quarter-note duration. Notice how we did not change anything for voice 2. The result is that voice 1 plays two notes while voice 2 plays the same note for the duration. We only have to specify something for our voice number if something changes, otherwise we just pass a -1 to let the computer know to play the next quarter-note duration of the tune.

LESSON 13 SOME MORE RANDOMNESS

So far, we have generally created programs that have predictable results in response to our exact instructions. However, often we need to make something happen at an unpredictable time or have an unpredictable result. For example, if we want to roll some dice, we want it to be essentially a random result. This is where the RND command comes in.

We have already briefly looked at the RND statement but let's look a bit deeper at what we can do with it. Try this very basic program to PRINT out the results of a RND statement:

```
10  PRINT CHR$(147);CHR$(5)
20  POKE 53280,4:POKE 53281,8
30  FOR I=1 TO 10
40  PRINT RND(0)
50  FOR T=1 TO 100:NEXT T
60  NEXT I
```

```
LIST

10 PRINT CHR$(147);CHR$(5)
20 POKE 53280,4:POKE 53281,8
30 FOR I=1 TO 10
40 PRINT RND(0)
50 FOR T=1 TO 100:NEXT T
60 NEXT I
READY.
```

```
.882815897
.550781965
.843751669
.378908873
.34765631
.152345002
.292971134
.183597267
.601563275
.839845479
READY.
```

The RND statement generates a random number between 0 and 1, but never exactly 0 or 1. Although we call RND a random function, this is not strictly true. We should really call this a pseudo-random function because it produces results according a predetermined sequence of numbers already stored in the computer. Think of it like a very long list of numbers already stored in the computer and calling the RND function allows us to get a value from this list in different ways so that the value is random enough for our purposes.

Calling RND by itself produces only decimal fractions between 0 and 1. What if you want a number between 0 and 10 instead? Let's change our code to do this.

Change line 40:

```
40 PRINT RND(0)*10
```

```
5.27346075
7.304703
.859383941
6.40625358
5.97659648
2.85158873
9.02345598
.820322633
.15625596
9.37500358
READY.
```

Now our numbers are decimal fractions between 0 and 10. What if we only want whole numbers between 0 and 10? We can use the INT function to convert our decimal fractions to whole numbers. Change line 40:

```
40 PRINT INT(RND(0)*10)
```

We can use the RND(0) statement to generate the numbers for a dice rolling program.

```
10 POKE 53280,4:POKE 53281,8:PRINT CHR$(147); CHR$(5);
20 FOR X=1 TO 10
30 PRINT CHR$(147);
40 D=INT(RND(0)*6)+1
50 IF D=1 THEN A=1:B=2:C=1
60 IF D=2 THEN A=2:B=1:C=2
70 IF D=3 THEN A=2:B=2:C=2
80 IF D=4 THEN A=3:B=1:C=3
90 IF D=5 THEN A=3:B=2:C=3
100 IF D=6 THEN A=3:B=3:C=3
110 PRINT "[SHFT+O][THEC64+Y][THEC64+Y][THEC64+Y]+[SHFT+P]"
120 IF A=1 THEN PRINT "[THEC64+H]    [THEC64+N]":GOTO 150
130 IF A=2 THEN PRINT "[THEC64+H][SHFT+Q]  [THEC64+N]":GOTO 150
140 IF A=3 THEN PRINT "[THEC64+H][SHFT+Q]  [SHFT+Q][THEC64+N]":GOTO
150
150 IF B=1 THEN PRINT "[THEC64+H]    [THEC64+N]":GOTO 180
160 IF B=2 THEN PRINT "[THEC64+H] [SHFT+Q] [THEC64+N]":GOTO 180
```

146

```
170 IF B=3 THEN PRINT "[THEC64+H][SHFT+Q] [SHFT+Q][THEC64+N]":GOTO
180
180 IF C=1 THEN PRINT "[THEC64+H]    [THEC64+N]":GOTO 210
190 IF C=2 THEN PRINT "[THEC64+H] [SHFT+Q][THEC64+N]":GOTO 210
200 IF C=3 THEN PRINT "[THEC64+H][SHFT+Q] [SHFT+Q][THEC64+N]":GOTO
210
210 PRINT "[SHFT+L][THEC64+P][THEC64+P][THEC64+P][SHIFT+@]"
220 FOR T=1 TO 400:NEXT T
230 NEXT X
```

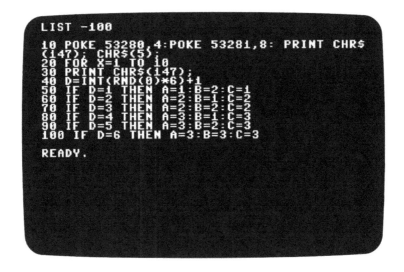

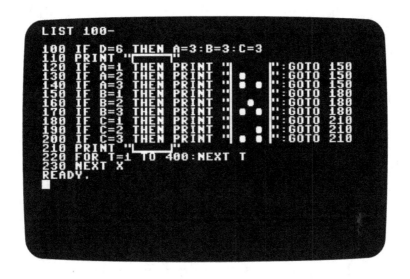

Much of the code should look very familiar to you by now as we set up colours, clear the screen and loop through the code 10 times. You can also see that line 40 uses the RND function to provide a random number between 1 and 6.

The remainder of the code is used to PRINT out the die face depending on what number was randomly provided. The first and last rows of the die face are going to stay the same no matter what number we have (see lines 110 and 210). However, the middle three rows of the die display will depend on what number was provided. If you inspect a die, you will see that for each row there are only three different possible combinations of dots. For example, the first row of dots can either be blank, a dot on the left or a dot on each side. By assigning each row of dots a letter (A, B or C) and each variation a number (1,2 or 3) we can define the appearance of the die face by assigning each row letter a number. Lines 50 to 100 define the values for A, B and C depending on what number we 'rolled'. Then lines 110 to 210 PRINT out the die face display based on these values.

Let's dig a bit deeper into what is possible with the RND function. You can give the RND statement one of three kinds of values depending on what you want it to do.

RND(<positive_number>): gives you the next number in the predetermined sequence.

RND(<negative_number>): jump to the position in the sequence specified by this particular negative number. Calling RND with the same negative number will produce the same result each time.

RND(0): generates a random number based on the value of the internal clock. This range of numbers is limited because the internal clock only produces digits in the range of 0 to 60. This method is not good for generating large ranges of numbers.

If you turn on your computer and call RND(1) a few times, you will get the exact same sequence of numbers each time because RND(1) starts at the beginning of the predetermined internal sequence of numbers.

So, you can use RND(0) to produce a good random number set, as long as you don't need many of them. However, if you really want a set of random numbers within a large range, we often combine a couple of steps to 'seed' our random number generator with a random starting point.

If we can call RND with an unpredictable and potentially large negative number, we will 'seed' our random sequence starting point and then call RND(1) to fetch a list of random numbers from there. The most common seed value to use is the system TIME variable, TI. This counts up from 0 to 5183999 every 1/60th of a second since you turned your computer on. This gives us a great 'seed' value to initialize our random number generator by calling RND(-TI) once and then calling RND(1) from thereon in.

Let's look at the difference between calling RND(0) and RND(1). We will use a short program that will fill the screen with asterisks in random positions. Since there are 1000 possible positions on the screen, we will generate a random integer between 0 and 1000. First, let's use RND(0).

```
10  PRINT CHR$(147)
20  POKE 53280,8:POKE 53281,9
30  FOR I=1 TO 1000
40  POKE 1024+INT(RND(0)*1000),42
50  NEXT I
```

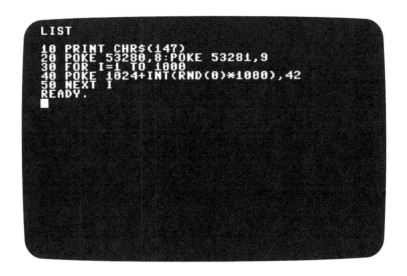

```
LIST

10 PRINT CHR$(147)
20 POKE 53280,8:POKE 53281,9
30 FOR I=1 TO 1000
40 POKE 1024+INT(RND(0)*1000),42
50 NEXT I
READY.
```

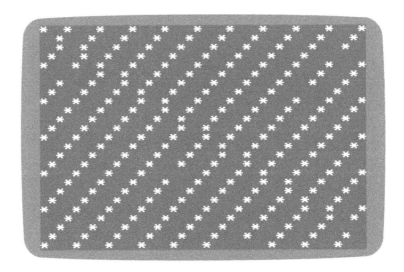

As you can see, the RND(0) statement produces a pattern of positions on the screen because it is limited in the range of possible numbers it can produce. If we need to produce a large range of numbers, like the 1000 we need to fill the screen, we must use RND(1) instead. Let's change line 40 to use RND(1) and run it again:

```
40 POKE 1024+INT(RND(1)*1000),42
```

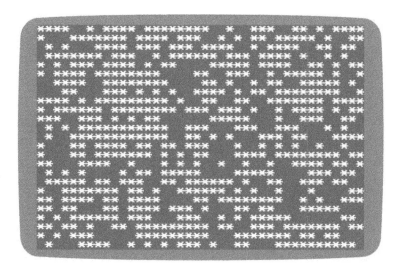

You can see that our random numbers cover the spectrum between 0 and 1000 (some spaces are not filled in because some positions are selected more than once). However, every time we restart the computer (which resets our random number sequence back to the start) and run this program, the screen will fill up with the asterisks in exactly the same order. To get a random order, we would need to first seed our random number generator with a random starting point. We could add in an extra line of code before our loop to use the TIME (TI) system variable to seed a random start point for our numbers.

```
25 X=RND(-TI)
```

LESSON 14 SUBROUTINES

So far, we have seen how we can repeat sections of code using loops like FOR …NEXT and GOTO loops. However, when our programs get larger, using GOTO statements to jump around our code can get messy and confusing resulting in what we call 'spaghetti code'. These maze-like programs can be almost impossible to maintain and troubleshoot. Instead, complex programs are written methodically using blocks or modules of code that can be run and tested independently of the others. Then when you put the entire program together, a main program will branch off to the various modules as is needed and when done, return to the main program again.

The Commodore 64 enables you to set aside blocks of code as subroutines that can be called using the GOSUB statement. For example:

```
80 GOSUB 400
```

The main program runs as normal until it reaches line 80. It then jumps, or branches off, to a subroutine that starts at line 400. When the subroutine is finished, it must end with the RETURN statement that will return the computer back to the next line of code in the main program, in this case line 90.

Subroutines are incredibly useful when you have programs that involve repetitive tasks, like calculations and animation. Let's try out a subroutine to simplify a program involving animation.

```
10 PRINT CHR$(147)
20 POKE 53280,0;POKE 53281,0
30 POKE 214,23;POKE 211,18
40 PRINT CHR$(30); CHR$(127); CHR$(184); CHR$(169);
50 X=INT(RND(0)*13)*3
```

```
60 PRINT CHR$(156):FOR Y=1 TO 22
70 POKE 214,Y-1:PRINT:POKE 211,X
80 PRINT " ":POKE 211,X
90 PRINT CHR$(171);CHR$(119);CHR$(179);
100 IF X=18 THEN IF Y=22 THEN GOSUB 500
110 FOR T=1 TO 5:NEXT T
120 NEXT Y:GOTO 50
500 FOR T=1 TO 20
510 POKE 214,22:PRINT:POKE 211,18
520 PRINT CHR$(28); CHR$(127); CHR$(184); CHR$(169)
530 POKE 214,22:PRINT:POKE 211,18
540 PRINT CHR$(30); CHR$(127); CHR$(184); CHR$(169)
550 NEXT T : RETURN
```

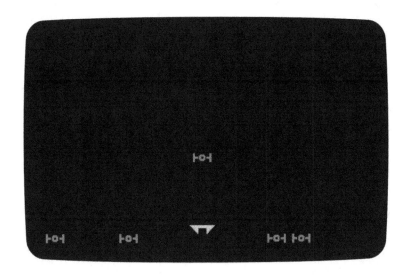

In this code we PRINT a green platform at the bottom of the screen (lines 30 and 40). Then lines 50 to 120 PRINTs a series of purple ships descending from random positions at the top of the screen. Line 100 checks to see if the current falling ship hits the platform. If it does, we call our subroutine at line 500.

This subroutine causes the platform to flash red and green for a moment before returning to the main program to begin all over again.

LESSON 15 PUT IT ALL TOGETHER

We have explored a range of amazing things that you can now program your own Commodore 64 to do. Using what we have learnt so far, we are going to create something that will bring together user input, colours, character graphics, music and sprites in one modular program. We are going to build it up incrementally by creating and testing individual subroutine modules. Finally, we will tie these modules together into a single main program workflow.

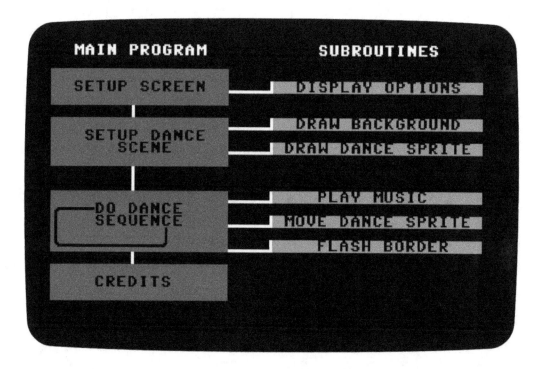

The overall plan is to create a series of subroutine modules as follows:

1. Display Options: Display the options available and store the results of our input from the user.

2. Draw Background: Display the background using character graphics.

3. Draw Dance Sprite: Draw the initial dancer sprite on the screen.

4. Play Music: Play the Dance of the Sugar Plum Fairy tune.

5. Move Dance Sprite: Animate the dancer sprite across the screen.

6. Flash Border: Animate the border colour.

Once we have created and tested these 6 subroutine modules individually, we will tie them together into the overall main program workflow.

1. Setup Screen: Set up the starting screen colours. Calls the Display Options subroutine once to collect user input.

2. Setup Dance Scene: Calls the Draw Background and Draw Dance Sprite subroutines to display the starting point for the dance.

3. Do Dance Sequence: Repeatedly calls the Play Music, Move Dance Sprite and Flash Border subroutines in a loop to perform the dance sequence.

4. Credits: Once the dance is over, display the closing credits for this program.

That's the plan. Let's begin with the first subroutine module.

DISPLAY OPTIONS

Our Display Options subroutine needs to display an opening screen that lets the user select a colour. We will use the colour selection to determine the colour of our dancer later in the program. Let's begin this subroutine at line number 500.

```
500 REM *** DISPLAY OPTIONS ***
```

```
510 PRINT CHR$(147); CHR$(28);
520 POKE 214,0:POKE 211,0:SYS 58732
530 FOR I=1 TO 400
540 PRINT CHR$(205.5+RND(1));
550 NEXT I
560 POKE 214,11:POKE 211,5:SYS 58732
570 PRINT CHR$(5);"DANCE OF THE SUGAR PLUM FAIRY"
580 POKE 214,14:POKE 211,8:SYS 58732
590 PRINT CHR$(28);"1-RED ";CHR$(156);"2-PURPLE ";CHR$(158);"3-
YELLOW ";
600 POKE 214,16:POKE 211,5:SYS 58732
610 PRINT CHR$(5);"SELECT A COLOUR TO BEGIN (1-3)"
620 C$=" ":C=0
630 GET C$:IF C$="" THEN GOTO 630
640 C=ASC(C$):IF (C>=49 AND C<=51) THEN GOTO 720
650 BF=15:GOSUB 2010
660 POKE 214,18:POKE 211,6:SYS 58732
670 PRINT CHR$(28);"PLEASE SELECT 1, 2 OR 3 ONLY"
680 FOR T=1 TO 100;NEXT T
690 POKE 214,18:POKE 211,6:SYS 58732
700 PRINT CHR$(155);"PLEASE SELECT 1, 2 OR 3 ONLY"
710 GOTO 630
720 BF=25:GOSUB 2010
730 END:REM RETURN
740 REM *** END DISPLAY OPTIONS ***
```

```
LIST 500-650

500 REM *** DISPLAY OPTIONS ***
510 PRINT CHR$(147);CHR$(28);
520 POKE 214,0:POKE 211,0:SYS 58732
530 FOR I=1 TO 400
540 PRINT CHR$(205.5+RND(1));
550 NEXT I
560 POKE 214,11:POKE 211,5:SYS 58732
570 PRINT CHR$(5);"DANCE OF THE SUGAR PL
UM FAIRY"
580 POKE 214,14:POKE 211,8:SYS 58732
590 PRINT CHR$(28);"1-RED ";CHR$(156);"2
-PURPLE ";CHR$(158);"3-YELLOW"
600 POKE 214,16:POKE 211,5:SYS 58732
610 PRINT CHR$(5);"SELECT A COLOUR TO BE
GIN (1-3)"
620 C$=" ":C=0
630 GET C$:IF C$="" THEN GOTO 630
640 C=ASC(C$):IF (C)=49 AND C<=51) THEN
GOTO 720
650 BF=15:GOSUB 2010

READY.
```

```
LIST 660-740

660 POKE 214,18:POKE 211,6:SYS 58732
670 PRINT CHR$(28);"PLEASE SELECT 1, 2 O
R 3 ONLY"
680 FOR T=1 TO 100:NEXT T
690 POKE 214,18:POKE 211,6:SYS 58732
700 PRINT CHR$(155);"PLEASE SELECT 1, 2
OR 3 ONLY"
710 GOTO 630
720 BF=25:GOSUB 2010
730 END:REM RETURN
740 REM *** END DISPLAY OPTIONS ***

READY.
```

Notice how we have used the REMark statement to mark out the divisions in our code. Use REM statements to provide information and commentary in your code as needed.

You will notice a new statement used with our POKE 214 and POKE 211 positioning statements – SYS 58732. This calls the in-built

Commodore 64 routine that sets the cursor position, placing the cursor exactly where you want to begin PRINTing your next output.

Let's look at what the code does. Line 510 clears the screen and sets the text colour to red. Line 520 positions the cursor to the very top left corner of the screen. Lines 530 to 550 loop through PRINTing 400 characters (10 lines) using a famous little line of code that PRINTs out random characters that form an ever-changing maze pattern. This just provides an interesting opening screen for our users.

Lines 560 to 610 PRINT our various text parts to screen, including a prompt for the user to select one of three colours by pressing the numbers 1, 2 or 3. We chose not to use the INPUT statement but instead use the new GET statement to read the current key being pressed on the keyboard. Line 630 loops through repeatedly until a key is pressed. Line 640 then check if the ASCII code of the key pressed is one of the numbers 1, 2 or 3 (ASCII codes 49, 50 or 51). If it is not one of these keys, lines 650 to 710 display a flashing 'error message' and then loops back to wait for a new key press. Look at line 650. This sets a numeric variable BF with a value and calls a subroutine located at line 2010. We will look at this in more detail, but basically this subroutine plays a short beep using the value to store in the variable BF as the frequency for the beep (BF stands for Beep Frequency).

If we did select a correct number, we drop down to line 720 to play a beep sound (using the subroutine). Line 730 is where we place our RETURN statement to end the Display Options subroutine and return to the main program. However, since we are only working on the subroutine itself, we use the END statement in conjunction with the REM statement so that the computer ignores the RETURN command and stops the program running instead. When we want to run this as part of the main program, we just remove the "END:REM" part.

Before you can run this code, you will also need to enter the Beep Sound subroutine.

```
2000 END:REM *** HELPER FUNCTIONS ***
2010 REM *** PLAY BEEP SOUND ***
2020 REM * REQUIRES BF, HIGH FREQ OF SOUND *
2030 S=54272
2040 FOR L=0 TO 24:POKE S+L,0:NEXT L
2050 POKE S+5,82:POKE S+6,195
2060 POKE S+3,8:POKE S+1,BF
2070 POKE S+4,65:POKE S+24,12
2080 FOR T=1 TO 50:NEXT T
2090 POKE S+4,64
2100 RETURN
```

The sound routine can be called at any time to play a short beep sound. We put this code into a subroutine so that we don't have to type out the same lines of code repeatedly through our code every time we want to play a beep. To make it even more versatile, we use a variable to specify the high value of the sound's frequency so that a large ranging of beep tones can be played from this one subroutine. The calling code has to give the variable BF a number before calling this subroutine to work.

Notice a few things you may have not seen before. Firstly, on line 2000, we begin with an END statement. This is to stop any possibility of the computer accidently running our helper subroutines. If for some reason the computer does end up at line 2000, it will simply end the program. Then on line 2040 we use a loop to completely reset all the memory registers controlling the SID (sound making) chip. We don't know what might have happened before this subroutine gets called so we reset all these values, so we know we are starting with a blank slate.

Now, since these two subroutines are the only ones in our code, we could just type the RUN command to run the code successfully. However, once we start adding extra subroutines in, we will need to specify the line numbers of the subroutine we want to test. So, let's start with a good habit and use the RUN command with the appropriate line number.

```
RUN 500
```

DRAW BACKGROUND

Our Draw Background subroutine needs to display the background that our dancing sprite will be placed on. We will use the Commodore 64's in-built character set to draw the stage on which our dancer will perform. Let's begin this subroutine at line number 800.

```
800 REM *** DRAW BACKGROUND ***
810 PRINT CHR$(147);
820 POKE 53280,0:POKE 53281,0
830 FOR I=0 TO 200
840 POKE 1024+800+I,160:POKE 55296+800+I,6
850 NEXT I
860 I=0
870 FOR X=3 TO 37 STEP 2
880 FOR Y=1 TO 19
890 CH=58:CL=2
900 IF I<1 THEN CH=46:CL=10
```

```
910 POKE 1024+Y*40+X,CH:POKE 55296+Y*40+X,CL
920 I=I+1:IF I>2 THEN I=0
930 NEXT Y
940 NEXT X
950 FOR X=0 TO 39
960 POKE 104+X,102:POKE 55296+X,2
970 NEXT X
980 FOR Y=1 TO 19:POKE 1024+Y*40+0,102: POKE 55296+Y*40+0,2:NEXT Y
990 FOR Y=1 TO 19:POKE 1024+Y*40+1,102: POKE 55296+Y*40+1,2:NEXT Y
1000 FOR Y=1 TO 4:POKE 1024+Y*40+2,102: POKE 55296+Y*40+2,2:NEXT Y
1010 FOR Y=1 TO 2:POKE 1024+Y*40+3,102: POKE 55296+Y*40+3,3:NEXT Y
1020 POKE 1024+Y*40+4,102: POKE 55296+Y*40+4,3
1030 POKE 1024+Y*40+5,102: POKE 55296+Y*40+5,3
1040 POKE 1024+Y*40+34,102: POKE 55296+Y*40+34,3
1050 POKE 1024+Y*40+35,102: POKE 55296+Y*40+35,3
1060 FOR Y=1 TO 2:POKE 1024+Y*40+36,102: POKE 55296+Y*40+36,3:NEXT
Y
1070 FOR Y=1 TO 4:POKE 1024+Y*40+37,102: POKE 55296+Y*40+37,3:NEXT
Y
1080 FOR Y=1 TO 19:POKE 1024+Y*40+38,102: POKE 55296+Y*40+38,3:NEXT
Y
1090 FOR Y=1 TO 19:POKE 1024+Y*40+39,102: POKE 55296+Y*40+39,3:NEXT
Y
1100 RETURN
```

```
LIST 800-940

800 REM *** DRAW BACKGROUND ***
810 PRINT CHR$(147);
820 POKE 53280,11:POKE 53281,0
830 FOR I=0 TO 200
840 POKE 1024+800+I,160:POKE 55296+800+I
,6
850 NEXT I
860 I=0
870 FOR X=3 TO 37 STEP 2
880 FOR Y=1 TO 19
890 CH=58:CL=2
900 IF I<1 THEN CH=46:CL=10
910 POKE 1024+Y*40+X,CH:POKE 55296+Y*40+
X,CL
920 I=I+1:IF I>2 THEN I=0
930 NEXT Y
940 NEXT X

READY.
■
```

```
LIST 950-1030

950 FOR X=0 TO 39
960 POKE 1024+X,102:POKE 55296+X,2
970 NEXT X
980 FOR Y=1 TO 19:POKE 1024+Y*40+0,102:P
OKE 55296+Y*40+0,2:NEXT Y
990 FOR Y=1 TO 19:POKE 1024+Y*40+1,102:P
OKE 55296+Y*40+1,2:NEXT Y
1000 FOR Y=1 TO 4:POKE 1024+Y*40+2,102:P
OKE 55296+Y*40+2,2:NEXT Y
1010 FOR Y=1 TO 2:POKE 1024+Y*40+3,102:P
OKE 55296+Y*40+3,2:NEXT Y
1020 POKE 1024+1*40+4,102:POKE 55296+1*4
0+4,2
1030 POKE 1024+1*40+5,102:POKE 55296+1*4
0+5,2

READY.
```

```
LIST 1040-1100

1040 POKE 1024+1*40+34,102:POKE 55296+1*
40+34,2
1050 POKE 1024+1*40+35,102:POKE 55296+1*
40+35,2
1060 FOR Y=1 TO 2:POKE 1024+Y*40+36,102:
POKE 55296+Y*40+36,2:NEXT Y
1070 FOR Y=1 TO 4:POKE 1024+Y*40+37,102:
POKE 55296+Y*40+37,2:NEXT Y
1080 FOR Y=1 TO 19:POKE 1024+Y*40+38,102
:POKE 55296+Y*40+38,2:NEXT Y
1090 FOR Y=1 TO 19:POKE 1024+Y*40+39,102
:POKE 55296+Y*40+39,2:NEXT Y
1100 RETURN

READY.
```

This subroutine basically draws a 'stage' on screen using a series of FOR … NEXT loops to POKE various characters and colours directly into the screen and colour memory. There are likely to be a number of ways we could streamline this subroutine, but let's keep it simple for now. To test this output, RUN the program starting at line 800.

RUN 800

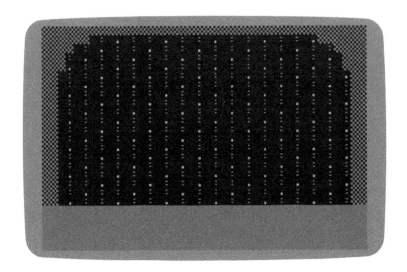

PLAY MUSIC

Our Play Music subroutine needs to play the song that our dancing sprite will dance to. We will re-use our music playing code from before. Firstly, let's enter out tune DATA statements beginning at line 5000.

```
5000 REM *** DATA ***
5010 REM *** MUSIC DATA ***
5020 REM * 147 BYTES *
5030 DATA 1,0,0,2,10,247,-1,-1
5040 DATA 1,52,38,2,13,10,-1,1,43,218,-1
5050 DATA 1,52,38,2,10,247,-1,-1
5060 DATA 1,49,57,2,14,162,-1,-1
5070 DATA 1,41,100,2,10,247,-1,-1
5080 DATA 1,43,218,2,15,129,-1,-1
5090 DATA 1,39,17,2,10,247,-1,1,39,17,-1
5100 DATA 1,39,17,2,16,109,-1,-1
```

```
5110 DATA 1,36,224,2,10,247,-1,1,36,224,-1
5120 DATA 1,36,224,2,18,112,-1,-1
5130 DATA 1,34,206,2,10,247,-1,1,34,206,-1
5140 DATA 1,34,206,2,19,137,-1,-1
5150 DATA 1,32,218,2,10,247,-1,1,43,218,-1
5160 DATA 1,34,206,2,10,247,-1,1,43,218,-1
5170 DATA 1,32,218,2,10,247,-1,-1
5180 DATA 1,0,0,2,0,0,-1,-1,-5
```

```
LIST 5000-5100

5000 REM *** DATA ***
5010 REM *** MUSIC DATA ***
5020 REM * 147 BYTES *
5030 DATA 1,0,0,2,10,247,-1,-1
5040 DATA 1,52,38,2,13,10,-1,1,43,218,-1

5050 DATA 1,52,38,2,10,247,-1,-1
5060 DATA 1,49,57,2,14,162,-1,-1
5070 DATA 1,41,100,2,10,247,-1,-1
5080 DATA 1,43,218,2,15,129,-1,-1
5090 DATA 1,39,17,2,10,247,-1,1,39,17,-1

5100 DATA 1,39,17,2,16,109,-1,-1

READY.
```

```
LIST 5110-
5110 DATA 1,36,224,2,10,247,-1,1,36,224,
-1
5120 DATA 1,36,224,2,18,112,-1,-1
5130 DATA 1,34,206,2,10,247,-1,1,34,206,
-1
5140 DATA 1,34,206,2,19,137,-1,-1
5150 DATA 1,32,218,2,10,247,-1,1,43,218,
-1
5160 DATA 1,32,218,2,10,247,-1,1,43,218,
-1
5170 DATA 1,32,218,2,10,247,-1,-1
5180 DATA 1,0,0,2,0,0,-1,-1,-5
READY.
■
```

Now we can enter in our Play Music subroutine, starting at line 1200.

```
1200 REM *** PLAY MUSIC ***

1210 REM * INIT, CALL ONCE, 1ST *

1220 S=54272:POKE S+24,15

1230 POKE S+5,0:POKE S+6,160: POKE S+12,0:POKE S+14,160

1290 RETURN

1300 REM ** PLAY, CALL FOR EACH NOTE **

1310 READ C

1320 IF C=-5 THEN RESTORE:GOTO 1310

1330 IF C=-1 THEN GOTO 1400

1340 READ H,L

1350 POKE S+(C*7)-3,32

1360 IF H=0 THEN GOTO 1310

1370 POKE S+(C*7)-7,L:POKE S+(C*7)-6,H

1380 POKE S+(C*7)-3,33

1390 GOTO 1310

1400 RETURN
```

171

```
LIST 1200-1400
1200 REM *** PLAY MUSIC ***
1210 REM * INIT, CALL ONCE, 1ST *
1220 S=54272:POKE S+24,15
1230 POKE S+5,0:POKE S+6,160:POKE S+12,0
:POKE S+13,160
1290 RETURN
1300 REM ** PLAY, CALL FOR EACH NOTE **
1310 READ C
1320 IF C=-5 THEN RESTORE:GOTO 1310
1330 IF C=-1 THEN GOTO 1400
1340 READ H,L
1350 POKE S+(C*7)-3,32
1360 IF H=0 THEN GOTO 1310
1370 POKE S+(C*7)-7,L:POKE S+(C*7)-6,H
1380 POKE S+(C*7)-3,33
1390 GOTO 1310
1400 RETURN

READY.
■
```

Our Play Music subroutine has two parts to it. Lines 1210 to 1290 initialise some variables and SID chip values and only needs to be called once by the main program.

The second part, from lines 1300 to 1400 play the next notes in the sequence. Whereas before we used a FOR … NEXT loop to loop through all of the notes and then end the program, in the subroutine we want to read and play the next set of notes in the sequence only. We will leave the looping through the tune in the hands of the main program. A couple of details had to be changed to get this working.

In order to keep the tune looping through once it reached the end, when the tune finish flag value of -5 is READ, instead of ENDing the program we RESTORE the DATA pointer back to the beginning of the song and start over again (line 1320). Otherwise, the code plays the notes as it did before, but instead of looping, it returns back to the main program. Each time this subroutine is called it plays the second part of the tune.

To test this subroutine, we can't just run it from line 1210. We need to create a short snippet of code that will test the functionality in a sensible way. This snippet will need to do the following steps:

1. Call the initialization part of the subroutine
2. Then loop through all the steps in the tune (there are 30) and call the play part of the sub routine. Don't forget to pause briefly between playing each sequence.

Type in the test snippet and RUN it.

```
10 GOSUB 1210
20 FOR X=0 TO 30
30 GOSUB 1300
40 FOR T=1 TO 50:NEXT T
50 NEXT X
60 END
```

```
LIST
10 PRINT CHR$(147)
20 FOR I=0 TO 15
30 POKE 53280,I : POKE 53281,I
40 FOR T=1 TO 1000 : NEXT T
50 NEXT I
READY.
```

DRAW DANCE SPRITE

The first step here is to design our dancer sprite. We also want to have a dancing animation, so we will need two versions of the sprite.

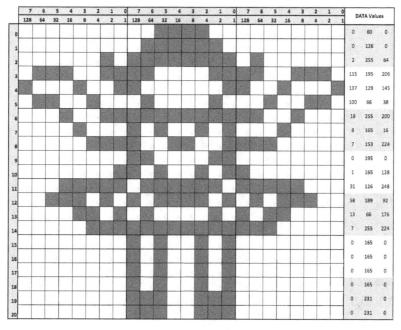

	DATA Values		
0	0	60	0
1	0	126	0
2	2	255	64
3	115	195	206
4	137	129	145
5	100	66	38
6	19	255	200
7	8	165	16
8	7	153	224
9	0	195	0
10	1	165	128
11	31	126	248
12	58	189	92
13	13	66	176
14	7	255	224
15	0	165	0
16	0	165	0
17	0	165	0
18	0	165	0
19	0	231	0
20	0	231	0

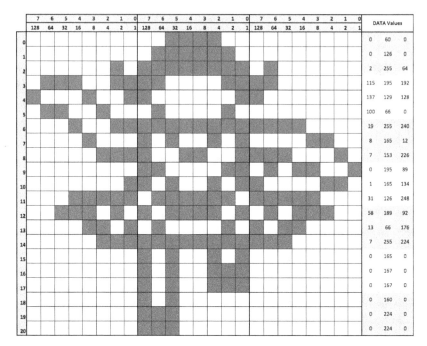

The idea is that as we move the sprite across the screen, we will switch between each version and therefore achieve a dancing ballerina on our stage.

Let's start by entering the DATA for our first sprite at line 5200.

```
5200 *** SPRITE 1 DATA ***
5210 * 64 BYTES *
5220 DATA 0,60,0,0,126,0,2,255,64
5230 DATA 115,195,206,137,129,145,100,66,38
5240 DATA 19,255,200,8,165,16,7,153,224
5250 DATA 0,195,0,1,165,128,31,126,248
5260 DATA 58,189,92,13,66,176,7,255,224
5270 DATA 0,165,0,0,165,0,0,165,0
5280 DATA 0,165,0,0,231,0,0,231,0,0
```

Now, if you examine the sprite data for both our sprites, you will see that only a few values are different between them. Instead of typing in another 62 bytes of data, we can simply type in the values that are different. There are two blocks of data that are different. In the first block we have bytes 11, 14, 17, 20, 23, 26, 29 and 33. The second block has bytes 49, 52, 55, 58 and 61. Notice how in each block, the bytes in increments of 3, very easily handled in a FOR … NEXT loop. Let's enter these two blocks of data.

```
5290 REM *** SPRITE 2 BLOCK 1 ***

5300 REM * 8 BYTES *

5310 DATA 192,128,0,240,12,226,89,134

5320 REM *** SPRITE 2 BLOCK 2 ***

5330 REM * 5 BYTES *

5340 DATA 167,167,160,224,224
```

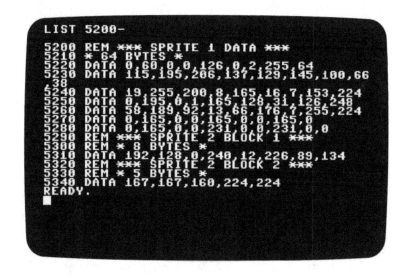

```
1410 REM *** DRAW DANCE SPRITE ***

1420 V=53248

1430 FOR SC=0 TO 146:READ BYTE:NEXT SC

1440 FOR SC=0 TO 63:READ BYTE

1450 POKE 832+SC,BYTE:POKE 896+SC,BYTE:NEXT SC
```

```
1460 FOR SC=11 TO 32 STEP 3:READ BYTE

1470 POKE 896+SC,BYTE:NEXT SC

1480 FOR SC=49 TO 61 STEP 3:READ BYTE

1490 POKE 896+SC,BYTE:NEXT SC

1500 POKE 2040,13:POKE V+39,1

1510 POKE V,173:POKE V+1,189: POKE V+16,0:POKE V+21,1

1520 SX=173:DX=2:SM=14:DS=1

1530 END:REM RETURN
```

```
LIST 1410-1530
1410 REM *** DRAW DANCE SPRITE ***
1420 V=53248
1430 FOR SC=0 TO 146:READ BYTES:NEXT SC
1440 FOR SC=0 TO 63:READ BYTE
1450 POKE 832+SC,BYTE:POKE 896+SC,BYTE:N
EXT SC
1460 FOR SC=11 TO 32 STEP 3:READ BYTE
1470 POKE 896+SC,BYTE:NEXT SC
1480 FOR SC=49 TO 61 STEP 3:READ BYTE
1490 POKE 896+SC,BYTE:NEXT SC
1500 POKE 2040,13:POKE V+39,1
1510 POKE V,173:POKE V+1,189:POKE V+16,0
:POKE V+21,1
1520 SX=173:DX=2:SM=14:DS=1
1530 END:REM RETURN

READY.
```

The code for the Draw Dance Sprite subroutine will read in the DATA for the two sprites, display the first sprite in the middle of the screen and set up some variables ready for the animation.

Line 1430 skips over the first 147 bytes of DATA. If you remember, these bytes of contain the tune DATA and so we need to skip past them to get to the sprite information. Then in lines 1440 and 1550 we read the first sprite data into the memory locations for both sprites.   This is because most of our second sprite data is identical to the first. Then lines 1460 to 1490 perform two loops that read the two different blocks of DATA for our second sprite and overwrite the data in our second sprite locations as needed.

Then lines 1500 and 1510 actually draw our first sprite in the middle of the screen. At the moment, we just draw our sprite using the white colour value. later, we will change the statement POKE 39,1 with a variable so that we can draw the sprite the colour the user selects in the options screen. Line 1520 sets up some variables required for the animation and line 1530 is where our RETURN statement will sit, at the moment we END the program so we can test this subroutine. Go ahead and run a test of this subroutine now:

```
RUN 1410
```

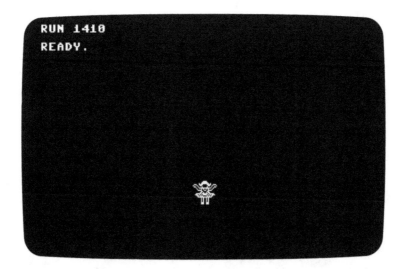

You should see your dancer sprite appear in the lower middle of the screen. When you want to erase this sprite from the screen, call the POKE statement with the memory address for sprite visibility and assign a value of 0 to turn all sprites off.

```
POKE 53269,0
```

When you have finished testing the subroutine, change line 1530 to remove our END statement and activate the RETURN statement:

```
1530 RETURN
```

Don't forget to save your program to disk.

MOVE DANCE SPRITE

Now it is time to code our subroutine to perform the movement and animation of our dancer across the screen. Begin our subroutine at line 1540.

```
1540 REM *** MOVE DANCE SPRITE ***
1550 DS=-DS
1560 IF SX<50 OR SX>280 THEN DX=-DX
1570 SM=SM+DS : SX=SX+DX
1580 T=INT(SX/256):POKE V+16,T
1590 POKE V,SX-T*256:POKE V+1,189
1600 POKE 2040,SM
1610 RETURN
```

```
LIST 1540-1610

1540 REM *** MOVE DANCE SPRITE ***
1550 DS=-DS
1560 IF SX<50 OR SX>280 THEN DX=-DX
1570 SM=SM+DS : SX=SX+DX
1580 T=INT(SX/256):POKE V+16,T
1590 POKE V,SX-T*256:POKE V+1,189
1600 POKE 2040,SM
1610 RETURN

READY.
```

We initialise (or set up) the variables we use to control our animation in our Draw Dance Sprite subroutine. We do this because we only call that subroutine once, and we call it before we use this Move Dance Sprite subroutine.

The variables are as follows:

1. SX: holds the X (horizontal) position of our dancer on the screen. We will increment or decrement this value to move our dancer left and right across the screen.

2. DX: is the amount we change SX by, either +2 (move 2 right) or -2 (move 2 left).

3. SM: the memory pointer of the sprite DATA we want to display. If we set this to 13, we display our first sprite, if we set it to 14, we display the second.

4. DS: we use this to switch between SM value of 13 and 14. We do this by switching it from +1 to -1 every time we call this subroutine.

Line 1550 switches the DS variable between +1 and -1 each time we call the subroutine. Line 1560 checks if our sprite is as far left or

180

far right as we want it to travel. If it is, then we switch DX to move the sprite in the opposite direction. Line 1570 changes the value of SX (so we can move our sprite either left or right) and SM (so we can animate our sprite).

Remember how we learned that if the X value of a sprite was greater that 256, we needed to start the X count back at 0 and set the X-MSB bit for that sprite? Well, line 1580 handles this requirement. If our X position is greater than 256, then the value of T will be 1, otherwise it will be 0. Since we only have one sprite on the screen, we can simply use the value of T for setting our X-MSB bit (V+16). Then line 1590 will set the X position of our sprite. Again, if it is larger than 256, we are supposed to start counting again from 0 and the formula here handles that for us. Finally, line 1600 switches the memory location for our sprite data to perform the animation and line 1610 returns us back to the main program.

Like it is with our music subroutine, we can't test this subroutine directly. We need to write a little test program to initialize the sprite using the Draw Dance Sprite subroutine and then repeatedly call the Move Dance Sprite subroutine within a FOR … NEXT loop. Again, type this in at line 10 (you may need to clear out your previous test code from our music subroutine test by typing in the line number followed by the RETURN key to clear that line). Notice how we call POKE V+21,0 just before we end the test code so that we erase the sprite from the screen.

RUN this code and you should see your sprite move and animate right and left across the screen rather quickly.

```
10 GOSUB 1410
20 FOR X=0 TO 200
30 GOSUB 1540
40 FOR T=1 TO 10:NEXT T
50 NEXT X
60 POKE V+21,0
```

70 END

```
LIST -100

10 GOSUB 1410
20 FOR X=0 TO 200
30 GOSUB 1540
40 FOR T=1 TO 10:NEXT T
50 NEXT X
60 POKE V+21,0
70 END

READY.
```

FLASH BORDER

Our last subroutine is the simplest of all. Every time we call the Flash Border subroutine, we want the border colour to change. Start this at line 1700.

```
1700 REM *** FLASH BORDER ***
1710 IF BC<0 OR BC>15 THEN BC=0
1720 POKE 53280,BC : BC=BC+1
1730 RETURN
```

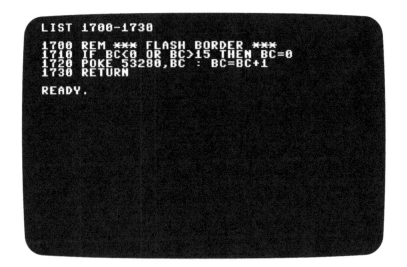

Line 1710 does double duty for us. We will use the variable BC to track and change our border colour between calls. The first time we run this subroutine, it will assign BC to 0 (black). Then every other time, it will reset BC to 0 once we pass the maximum value for our border colour, 15. Line 1520 changes the border colour and increments our border colour value before returning to the main program.

183

Again, we will need a short piece of code to test our subroutine in a loop.

```
10 FOR X=1 TO 100
20 GOSUB 1700
30 FOR T=1 TO 80:NEXT T
40 NEXT X
50 END
```

```
LIST -100
10 FOR X=1 TO 100
20 GOSUB 1700
30 FOR T=1 TO 80:NEXT T
40 NEXT X
50 END
READY.
```

RUN this code to see the border change.

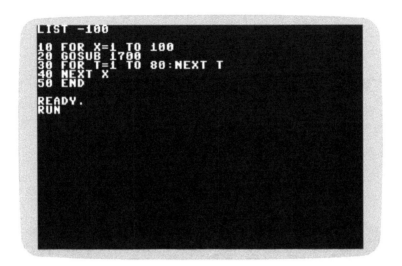

```
LIST -100

10 FOR X=1 TO 100
20 GOSUB 1700
30 FOR T=1 TO 80:NEXT T
40 NEXT X
50 END

READY.
RUN
```

185

THE MAIN PROGRAM

Now that we have all our subroutine functionality written, we can now tie this all together into our main program.

```
10 REM *** MAIN PROGRAM ***
20 POKE 53280,0:POKE 53281,0
30 GOSUB 500
40 CO=2
50 IF C$="2" THEN CO=4:GOTO 70
60 IF C$="3" THEN CO=7
70 GOSUB 800
80 GOSUB 1410
90 GOSUB 1200
100 RESTORE
110 FOR I=1 TO 200
120 GOSUB 1300
130 GOSUB 1540
140 GOSUB 1700
150 FOR T=1 TO 30:NEXT T
160 NEXT I
170 POKE 54276,32:POKE 54283,32
180 POKE 214,21:POKE 211,12:SYS 58732
190 PRINT CHR$(18);CHR$(31);"BROUGHT TO YOU BY";
200 POKE 214,22:POKE 211,5:SYS 58732
210 PRINT "RICH STALS THE RETRO TECH GUY";
220 POKE 214,23:POKE 211,20:SYS 58732
230 PRINT "&";
240 POKE 214,24:POKE 211,16:SYS 58732
250 PRINT "YOUR NAME";
260 E$=" "
270 GET E$:IF E$="" THEN GOTO 270
```

```
280 POKE 53269,0
290 POKE 53280,0:POKE 53281,0:PRINT CHR$(147);CHR$(5);
300 END
```

```
LIST -160

10 REM *** MAIN PROGRAM ***
20 POKE 53280,0:POKE 53281,0
30 GOSUB 500
40 CO=2
50 IF C$="2" THEN CO=4:GOTO 70
60 IF C$="3" THEN CO=7
70 GOSUB 800
80 GOSUB 1410
90 GOSUB 1200
100 RESTORE
110 FOR I=1 TO 200
120 GOSUB 1300
130 GOSUB 1540
140 GOSUB 1700
150 FOR T=1 TO 30:NEXT T
160 NEXT I

READY.
```

```
LIST 170-300

170 POKE 54276,32:POKE 54283,32
180 POKE 214,21:POKE 211,12:SYS 58732
190 PRINT CHR$(18);CHR$(31);"BROUGHT TO
YOU BY";
200 POKE 214,22:POKE 211,5:SYS 58732
210 PRINT "RICH STALS THE RETRO TECH GUY
";
220 POKE 214,23:POKE 211,20:SYS 58732
230 PRINT "&";
240 POKE 214,24:POKE 211,16:SYS 58732
250 PRINT "YOUR NAME";
260 E$=""
270 GET E$:IF E$="" THEN GOTO 270
280 POKE 53269,0
290 POKE 53280,0:POKE 53281,0:PRINT CHR$
(147);CHR$(5);
300 END

READY.
```

In line 20 we set up the screen with a black border and black background. Then in line 30 we call the Display Options

187

subroutine. This will assign the string variable C$ with the user's choice of colour. Then, in lines 40-60 we process the colour choice and translate that into the correct number value for the colour code and assign that to the numeric variable CO.

Lines 70-90 call the Draw Background, Draw Dance Sprite and Music Initialisation subroutines. In order to use our new colour code, CO, we need to change a line in our Draw Dance Sprite subroutine. Change line 1500 to:

```
1500 POKE 2040,13:POKE V+39,CO
```

We also need to change this subroutine to perform a RETURN statement and not the END statement we currently have it set to. Change line 1530 to:

```
1530 RETURN
```

Now our Dancer is ready to go.

```
RUN
```

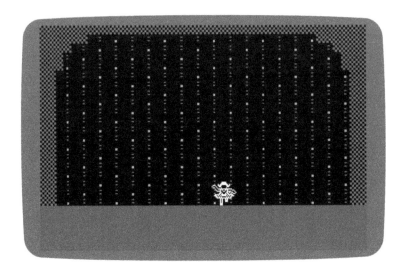

Line 100 calls the RESTORE statement that resets the DATA read pointer to the beginning of the list of DATA statements. We need to make sure that we start the next section at the beginning, where the DATA for the tune resides.

Lines 110 to 160 hold the loop that controls the playing of the tune, the movement and animation of the sprite and the flashing of the border. We have set it to repeat 200 times (line 110). Then on lines 120 to 150 we call the Play Music, Move Dance Sprite and Flash Border subroutines in order. This will play one note of our tune, move and animate the sprite one step and change the border colour once. Then line 150 performs a short pause. We use this to slow down our animation and tune to a speed that looks and sounds normal (not too fast or slow).

Once our dancer has repeated the dance moves 200 times back and forth across the screen, we need to make sure that we end the program in a graceful way. Without the following lines of code, the computer will continue to display the sprite on screen, continue to play the last note indefinitely and simply write the READY prompt over the top of whatever existing images we have displayed.

Instead, we want to silence any sound, display some text credits and pause the program until the user hits any key on the keyboard. Once they do, we will reset the screen completely. Let's examine each step of this process.

Line 170 stops the SID chip voices 1 and 2 playing any sound. Then lines 180 to 250 display the text credits at the bottom of the screen. Notice how we PRINT the control character to reverse the text, CHR$(18), so that it matches the 'stage' area of our screen. Don't forget to change line 250 to display your name.

Lines 260 and 270 pause the program by looping until the user presses any key on the keyboard. Once they do, lines 280 turns the sprite display off and line 290 resets the background and border to black, clears the screen and sets the cursor colour to white. When line 300 ENDs the execution of our program, the user is given a clear screen to continue using their computer.

Congratulations! You are now well on your way to becoming an 8-bit coding guru. Go ahead, plan and code a program of your own using what you have learned in this course. I can't wait to see what you create.

APPENDIX A ASCII CHARACTER SET

ASCII Code	Character	ASCII Code	Character	ASCII Code	Character	ASCII Code	Character
0		64	ℭ	128		192	▬
1		65	A	129	Orange	193	♣
2		66	B	130		194	▮
3	STOP	67	C	131	RUN	195	▬
4		68	D	132		196	▬
5	White	69	E	133	F1	197	▬
6		70	F	134	F3	198	▬
7		71	G	135	F5	199	▮
8		72	H	136	F7	200	▮
9		73	I	137	F2	201	◣
10		74	J	138	F4	202	◣
11		75	K	139	F6	203	◢
12		76	L	140	F8	204	◣
13	RETURN	77	M	141	SHIFT+RETURN	205	◥
14	Lower Case	78	N	142	Upper Case	206	◢
15		79	O	143		207	◤
16		80	P	144	Black	208	◥
17	Cursor Down	81	Q	145	Cursor Up	209	◉
18	Reverse On	82	R	146	Reverse Off	210	▬

ASCII Code	Character	ASCII Code	Character	ASCII Code	Character	ASCII Code	Character
19	HOME	83	S	147	CLR	211	♥
20	DEL	84	T	148	INS	212	▎
21		85	U	149	Brown	213	╭
22		86	V	150	Light Red	214	╳
23		87	W	151	Dark Grey	215	▢
24		88	X	152	Grey	216	✛
25		89	Y	153	Light Green	217	▏
26		90	Z	154	Light Blue	218	◆
27		91	[	155	Light Grey	219	✛
28	Red	92	£	156	Purple	220	⣿
29	Cursor Right	93	]	157	Cursor Left	221	▏
30	Green	94	↑	158	Yellow	222	⫟
31	Blue	95	←	159	Cyan	223	◣
32	SPACE	96	─	160	SHIFT+SPACE	224	
33	!	97	♠	161	▌	225	▌
34	"	98	│	162	▬	226	▬
35	#	99	─	163		227	
36	$	100	─	164	─	228	─
37	%	101	─	165	▍	229	▍
38	&	102	─	166	▨	230	▨
39	'	103	│	167	▐	231	▐
40	(	104	│	168	⠤	232	⠤
41	)	105	╮	169	◤	233	◤

195

ASCII Code	Character	ASCII Code	Character	ASCII Code	Character	ASCII Code	Character
42	✳	106	◣	170	▮	234	▮
43	✚	107	◢	171	┣	235	┣
44	▪	108	◣	172	▪	236	▪
45	—	109	◥	173	◰	237	◰
46	▪	110	◢	174	◥	238	◥
47	╱	111	◰	175	▬	239	▬
48	0	112	◳	176	◰	240	◰
49	1	113	●	177	┻	241	┻
40	2	114	▬	178	┳	242	┳
51	3	115	♥	179	┫	243	┫
52	4	116	▮	180	▮	244	▮
53	5	117	◞	181	▮	245	▮
54	6	118	✕	182	▮	246	▮
55	7	119	◻	183	▬	247	▬
56	8	120	✥	184	▬	248	▬
57	9	121	▮	185	▬	249	▬
58	∶	122	◆	186	◳	250	◳
59	;	123	✚	187	▪	251	▪
60	❮	124	⁞	188	▪	252	▪
61	=	125	▮	189	◢	253	◢
62	❯	126	ᴨ	190	▪	254	▪
63	?	127	◣	191	◪	255	ᴨ

APPENDIX B SCREEN MEMORY CODES

Screen Code (Normal / Reverse)		Character (Upper / Lower)		Screen Code (Normal / Reverse)		Character (Upper / Lower)	
0	128	@		64	192	▬	
1	129	A	a	65	193	♣	A
2	130	B	b	66	194	▮	B
3	131	C	c	67	195	▬	C
4	132	D	d	68	196	▬	D
5	133	E	e	69	197	▬	E
6	134	F	f	70	198	▬	F
7	135	G	g	71	199	▮	G
8	136	H	h	72	200	▮	H
9	137	I	i	73	201	◥	I
10	138	J	j	74	202	◢	J
11	139	K	k	75	203	◣	K
12	140	L	l	76	204	⌐	L
13	141	M	m	77	205	◆	M
14	142	N	n	78	206	◢	N
15	143	O	o	79	207	⌐	O
16	144	P	p	80	208	⌐	P
17	145	Q	q	81	209	●	Q
18	146	R	r	82	210	—	R
19	147	S	s	83	211	♥	S

201

Screen Code (Normal / Reverse)		Character (Upper / Lower)		Screen Code (Normal / Reverse)		Character (Upper / Lower)	
20	148	T	t	84	212		T
21	149	U	u	85	213		U
22	150	V	v	86	214		U
23	151	W	w	87	215		W
24	152	X	x	88	216		X
25	153	Y	y	89	217		Y
26	154	Z	z	90	218		Z
27	155		[	91	219		
28	156		£	92	220		
29	157		]	94	221		
30	158		↑	94	222		
31	159		←	95	223		
32	160	SPACE		96	224	SPACE	
33	161		!	97	225		
34	162		"	98	226		
35	163		#	99	227		
36	164		$	100	228		
37	165		%	101	229		
38	166		&	102	230		
39	167		'	103	231		
40	168		(	104	232		
41	169		)	105	233		
42	170		✳	106	234		

Screen Code (Normal / Reverse)		Character (Upper / Lower)	Screen Code (Normal / Reverse)		Character (Upper / Lower)
43	171	✚	107	235	⊢
44	172	⌐	108	236	■
45	173	—	109	237	∟
46	174	■	110	238	⌐
47	175	╱	111	239	—
48	176	0	112	240	⌐
49	177	1	113	241	⊥
50	178	2	114	242	⊤
51	179	3	115	243	⊣
52	180	4	116	244	│
53	181	5	117	245	│
54	182	6	118	246	│
55	183	7	119	247	—
56	184	8	120	248	▬
57	185	9	121	249	▬
58	186	:	122	250	⌐ ╱
59	187	;	123	251	■
60	188	<	124	252	■
61	189	=	125	253	⌐
62	190	>	126	254	■
63	191	?	127	255	⌐

APPENDIX C ERROR MESSAGES

BAD DATA
String data was received from an open file, but the program was expecting numeric data.

BAD SUBSCRIPT
The program was trying to reference an element of an array whose number is outside of the range specified in the DIM statement.

BREAK
Program execution was stopped because you hit the <STOP> key.

CAN'T CONTINUE
The CONT command will not work, either because the program was never RUN, there has been an error, or a line has been edited.

DEVICE NOT PRESENT
The required I/O device was not available for an OPEN, CLOSE, CMD, PRINT#, INPUT#, or GET#.

DIVISION BY ZERO
Division by zero is a mathematical oddity and not allowed.

EXTRA IGNORED
Too many items of data were typed in response to an INPUT statement. Only the first few items were accepted.

FILE NOT FOUND
If you were looking for a file on tape, and END-OF-TAPE marker was found. If you were looking on disk, no file with that name exists.

FILE NOT OPEN
The file specified in a CLOSE, CMD, PRINT#, INPUT#, or GET#, must first be OPENed.

FILE OPEN
An attempt was made to open a file using the number of an already open file.

FORMULA TOO COMPLEX
The string expression being evaluated should be split into at least two parts for the system to work with, or a formula has too many parentheses.

ILLEGAL DIRECT
The INPUT statement can only be used within a program, and not in direct mode.

ILLEGAL QUANTITY
A number used as the argument of a function or statement is out of the allowable range.

LOAD
There is a problem with the program on tape.

NEXT WITHOUT FOR
This is caused by either incorrectly nesting loops or having a variable name in a NEXT statement that doesn't correspond with one in a FOR statement.

NOT INPUT FILE
An attempt was made to INPUT or GET data from a file which was specified to be for output only.

NOT OUTPUT FILE
An attempt was made to PRINT data to a file which was specified as input only.

OUT OF DATA
A READ statement was executed but there is no data left unREAD in a DATA statement.

OUT OF MEMORY
There is no more RAM available for program or variables. This may also occur when too many FOR loops have been nested, or when there are too many GOSUBs in effect.

OVERFLOW
The result of a computation is larger than the largest number allowed, which is 1.70141884E+38.

REDIM'D ARRAY
An array may only be DIMensioned once. If an array variable is used before that array is DIM'D, an automatic DIM operation is performed on that array setting the number of elements to ten, and any subsequent DIMs will cause this error.

REDO FROM START
Character data was typed in during an INPUT statement when

numeric data was expected. Just re-type the entry so that it is correct, and the program will continue by itself.

RETURN WITHOUT GOSUB
RETURN statement was encountered, and no GOSUB command has been issued.

STRING TOO LONG
A string can contain up to 255 characters.

?SYNTAX ERROR
A statement is unrecognizable by the Commodore 64. A missing or extra parenthesis, misspelled keywords, etc.

TYPE MISMATCH
This error occurs when a number is used in place of a string, or vice-versa.

UNDEF'D FUNCTION
A user defined function was referenced, but it has never been defined using the DEF FN statement.

UNDEF'D STATEMENT
An attempt was made to GOTO or GOSUB or RUN a line number that doesn't exist.

VERIFY
The program on tape or disk does not match the program currently in memory.

www.ingramcontent.com/pod-product-compliance
Lightning Source LLC
LaVergne TN
LVHW081523050326
832903LV00025B/1609